TAX REFORMS, DEMONITIZATION AND CASHLESS ECONOMY

TAX REFORMS, DEMONITIZATION AND CASHLESS ECONOMY

A Strategy for Economic Development of India

By
Dr. Rajib Mallik
Dr. Sukanta Sarkar

KALPAZ

First Published, 2018

Published by

Kalpaz Publications
C-30, Satyawati Nagar,
Delhi – 110052
Ph.: 011-47034999, 9811692060
www.kalpazpublications.com
E-mail: kalpaz@hotmail.com

Printed at: G. Print Process, Delhi

Cataloging in Publication Data—DK
Courtesy: D.K. Agencies (P) Ltd. <docinfo@dkagencies.com>

Malik, Rajib, author.
Tax reforms, demonetization and cashless economy : a strategy for economic development of India / by Dr. Rajib Malik, Dr. Sukanta Sarkar.
pages cm
Includes bibliographical references.
ISBN 9789386397997 (hardback)

1. Economic development—Government policy—India. 2. Value-added tax—India. 3. Monetary policy—India. 4. Electronic funds transfers—India. I. Sarkar, Sukanta, author. II. Title.

LCC HC435.3.M35 2018 | DDC 338.954 23

Contents

PART - II
DEMONITIZATION

PART - III
CASHLESS ECONOMY

Preface

Tax is a mandatory financial charge or some other type of levy imposed upon a taxpayer by a governmental organization in order to fund various public expenditures.The levying of taxes aims to raise revenue to fund governing and/or to alter prices in order to affect demand. States and their functional equivalents throughout history have used money provided by taxation to carry out many functions.Demonetization is the act of stripping a currency unit of its status as legal tender. It is necessary whenever there is a change of national currency.Cashless Economy is situation in which the flow of cash within an economy is non-existent and all transactions must be through electronic channels.

We desire to express our heartiest thank to Prof. B.K. Panda, Department of Economics, Berhampur University, Odisha who despite his busy schedule and hectic academic engagements, all the time encouraged and supported us. We have also beholden to Dr. N.G. Pendse, Department of Economics, Rani Durgabati University, Jabalpur who's erudite and scholarly tidbits for preparing such a vast work are still fresh in our mind. We also thanks to Dr. Pradeep Kumar Pandey, Centre of Judicial Studies, Dibrugarh University, Assam, Dr. Rakesh Joshi, Department of Economics, Saurashtra University, Gujarat; Dr. D. Pulla Rao, Department of Economics, Andhra University; Dr. Vibhuti Patel, Professor cum Director, Centre for Study of Social Exclusion and Inclusive Policy, SNDT Women's University, Mumbai; Dr.WakarAmin, Department of Social Work, University of Kashmir, J & K.; Dr.Shazia Manzoor, Assistant professor Department of Social Work, University of Kashmir, J & K; Dr. Pallab Kanti Ghoshal, Department of Commerce, BBM. College, Udaipur, for their valuable suggestions and moral support.

We are heartily grateful to Dr. Suman Kalan Chaudhury, Department of Business Administration, Berhampur University, Odisha; who always encouraged us to carry on this constructive work. Further, we express our heartily thankfulness to each and every person who directly/indirectly helped us in preparing this work. It is hoped that this book will be very useful society in general and students of social sciences in particular. Comments and suggestions are most welcomed.

Dr. Rajib Mallik
Dr. Sukanta Sarkar

Abbreviations

AEPS : Aadhaar-Enabled Payments System

ATM : Automatic Teller Machine

BC : Business Correspondents

BJP : Bharatiya Janata Party

CBS : Core Banking Solution

CIDA : Canadian International Development Agency

CST : Central Sales Tax

DCCB : District Central Cooperative Bank

ECS : Electronic Clearing Service

EPR : Electronic Payments and Receipts

FICN : Fake Indian Currency Notes

GDP : Gross Domestic Product

GST : Goods and Services Tax

GSTN : Goods and Services Tax Network

HUF : Hindu Undivided Families

ICT : Information and Communications Technology

IDRBT : Institute for Development and Research in Banking Technology

IGST : Integrated Goods and Service Tax

IMPS : Immediate Payment Service

ITC : Input Tax Credit

MMP : Mission Mode Project

MODVAT: Modified Value Added Tax

MoF : Ministry of Finance

NACH : National Automated Clearing House

NECS : National Electronic Clearing Service

NEFT : National Electronic Funds Transfer

NeGP : National eGovernance Plan

NFS : National Financial Switch

NREGA : National Rural Employment Guarantee Act

OTP : One Time Password

PACS : Primary Agricultural Credit Societies

PAN : Permanent Account Number

PDA : Personal Digital Assistant

PMJDY : Pradhan Mantri Jan Dhan Yojana

POS : Point-of-Sale

RBI : Reserve Bank of India

RTGS : Real Time Gross Settlement

TCS : Tax Collection at Source

UPI : Unified Payments Interface

USSD : Unstructured Supplementary Service Data

VAT : Value Added Tax

PART - I
TAX REFORMS

Chapter - 1

Taxation: An Overview

A tax is a mandatory financial charge or some other type of levy imposed upon a taxpayer (an individual or other legal entity) by a governmental organization in order to fund various public expenditures. A failure to pay, or evasion of or resistance to taxation, is punishable by law. The levying of taxes aims to raise revenue to fund governing and/or to alter prices in order to affect demand. States and their functional equivalents throughout history have used money provided by taxation to carry out many functions. When expenditures exceed tax revenue, a government accumulates debt. A portion of taxes may be used to service past debts. Governments also use taxes to fund welfare and public services.

The concept of tax was initiated from Great Britain in 1799 to collect revenue for the government to manage the war against France. It didn't come into practice after that for a long time. Income tax system was regularly begun from 1840 onwards in different countries in the world. It was begun from 1840 in Switzerland, 1849 in Austria, 1860 in England and Hindustan, 1862 in USA, 1864 in Italy and 1959 in Nepal as a regular source of government revenue.

Features of Tax

Important features of tax are:

- A tax is a compulsory contribution of a person or entity to the state as per the rules.
- The tax payer does not receive direct and or special benefit in return.

- It is spent by the government for the common interest and benefit of the people.
- It is paid only by those persons and entities who earns income exceeding a certain specified limit (Chimoriya, 2018).

Objectives of Taxation

The primary purpose of taxation is to raise revenue to meet huge public expenditure. Most governmental activities must be financed by taxation. In the modern world, taxation is used as an instrument of economic policy.

- Taxation helps in economic development. Economic development of any country is largely conditioned by the growth of capital formation. To step up both public and private investment, government taps tax revenues. The tax policy has to be employed in such a way that investment occurs in the productive sectors of the economy, including the infrastructural sectors.
- Second objective is the full employment. Since the level of employment depends on effective demand, a country desirous of achieving the goal of full employment must cut down the rate of taxes.
- Taxation can be used to ensure price stability. Taxes are regarded as an effective means of controlling inflation.
- It helps for control of cyclical fluctuations. During depression, taxes are lowered down while during boom taxes are increased so that cyclical fluctuations are tamed.
- Taxes like custom duties are used to control imports of certain goods help for reducing the intensity of balance of payments.
- It helps for reduction of inequalities in income and wealth (Mulay, 2017).

Canon of Taxation

Canons of taxation we simply mean the characteristics or qualities which a good tax system should possess. In fact, canons of taxation are related to the administrative part of a tax. Adam Smith first devised the principles or canons of taxation in 1776. He identifies four canons:

- Canon of Equality: Canon of equality states that the burden of taxation must be distributed equally or equitably among the taxpayers. Justice demands that a person having greater ability to pay must pay large taxes. If everyone is asked to pay taxes according to his ability, then sacrifices of all taxpayers become equal.

- Canon of Certainty: According to A. Smith, the time of payment, the manner of payment, the quantity to be paid, i.e., tax liability, ought all to be clear and plain to the contributor and to everyone. It must be certain to the taxpayer as well as to the tax-levying authority.
- Canon of Economy: According to A. Smith: "Every tax ought to be contrived as both to take out and to keep out of the pockets of the people as little as possible, over and above what it brings into the public treasury of the State." This canon implies that the cost of collecting a tax should be as minimum as possible.
- Canon of Convenience: "Every tax", stresses A. Smith: "ought to be levied at time or the manner in which it is most likely to be convenient for the contributor to pay it." Taxes should be levied and collected in such a manner that it provides the greatest convenience not only to the taxpayer but also to the government.

Characteristics of Canons of Taxation

A good tax system has to fulfil the following characteristics:

- The distribution of tax burden should be equitable such that every person is made to pay his 'fair share'.
- Equity must not hamper productive efficiency such that burdens should be provided to correct inefficiencies.
- A good tax system demands changes in tax rates whenever circumstances change the system. Further, a good tax must be transparent in the sense that taxpayers should know what they are paying for the services they are getting.
- A good tax system is expected to facilitate the use of fiscal policy to achieve the goals of (a) stability, and (b) economic growth (Muley, 2017).

Tax systems fall into three main categories within the tax code: regressive, proportional and progressive taxes. Regressive taxes are those that have a greater impact on low-income individuals than high-income earners. A proportional tax, also referred to as a flat tax, impacts low-, middle- and high-income earners relatively equally. A progressive tax has more of a financial impact on higher-income individuals and businesses, and less on low-income earners.

Proportional Tax

A proportional tax system assesses the same tax rate regardless of income or wealth. It is meant to create equality between marginal tax rate and average tax rate paid. Proponents of proportional taxes believe they stimulate the economy more by encouraging people to work more, as well as spend more. They also believe businesses are likely to spend and invest more as well under a flat tax system, putting more dollars into the economy. Some specific examples of proportional taxes include per capita taxes, gross receipts taxes, and occupational taxes. Such tax also referred to as a flat tax system.

Progressive Tax

Under a progressive tax system, the taxes assessed are based on the taxable amount, and follow an accelerating schedule. High-income earners pay more than low-income earners, and the tax rate, along with tax liability, increases as an individual or entity's wealth increases. The overall outcome is that higher earners pay a higher per centage of taxes and more money in taxes than do lower-income earners.Estate taxes are example of progressive taxes, as they mainly effect on high net worth individuals, and rise with the size of the estate.

Regressive Tax

Under a regressive tax system, individuals and entities with low incomes pay a higher amount of that income in taxes compared to high-income earners. Rather than basing the tax on the individual or entity's earnings or income level, the government assesses tax as a per centage of the asset that the taxpayer purchases or owns.Aside from state and local sales taxes, regressive taxes include real estate property taxes and excise taxes.

Tax Base

Tax base is defined as the income or asset balance used to calculate a tax liability, and the tax liability formula is tax base multiplied by tax rate. The rate of tax imposed varies depending on the type of tax and the tax base total. Income tax, gift tax and estate tax are each calculated using a different tax rate schedule.

Tax-Tolerance

It is the amount of tax that a population is willing to tolerate and put up with. In the western world there are strong political movements to resist higher tax and commit to lower tax rates.The tolerance to tax may also be determined by what the government is perceived to be spending money on. For example, during wars, tax rates usually rise to finance the cost of war.Western Europe has a greater tolerance to higher taxes because health care systems are largely publically funded and free at the point of use.

Direct Taxes

In general, a direct tax is one imposed upon an individual person (juristic or natural) or property (i.e. real and personal property, livestock, crops, wages, etc.) as distinct from a tax imposed upon a transaction. The distinction between direct and indirect taxation was first extensively discussed by Adam Smith in his Wealth of Nations, as in the following passage: "It is thus that a tax upon the necessaries of life operates exactly in the same manner as a direct tax upon the wages of labour. ... if he is a manufacturer, will charge upon the price of his goods this rise of wages, together with a profit; so that the final payment of the tax, together with this overcharge, will fall upon the consumer."

Types of Direct Tax

• Income Tax

Income tax is charged under the Indian Income Tax Act, 1961. It is an annual tax on income of both individuals and companies levied by the union government. Every person (individuals, Hindu undivided families, companies, firms, association of persons or bodies of individuals and all other artificial juridical persons), whose total income exceeds the maximum exemption limit, is chargeable to the income tax at the rates prescribed in the Finance Act passed each year by the parliament. The income tax is paid on the total income of an individual, determined on the basis of her/his residential status in India. In the taxable income are included the following heads: salaries; income from house property (determined by reference to the annual value of property); profits and gains of business or profession; capital gains; income from other sources (included interest) (Bernardi & Fraschini, 2005).

Income tax is a separate issue from sales tax when you're running a small business. Income tax is the amount you pay on your total income from the business to the federal and state government. Sales tax is a per centage amount that your customers have to pay when they purchase certain items from your business.Sales tax is the tax on the sale or lease of goods, and is what is known as a "pass-through tax." Unlike income tax, sales taxes is decided and administered by state governments only. Merchants are required to collect sales tax from their customers and remit it back to the state, essentially acting as tax collectors.Both are entirely different from each another. The main difference between income tax and sales tax is that income tax is a direct tax whose impact cannot be passed over to other persons while sales tax is an in direct tax whose impact always passed over to other persons like customers.

There are also various merit and demerit of income tax. Merit of income tax are: (a) An income tax is a rate charged on the income of individuals as well as business (companies or other legal entities). Individual income taxes often tax the total earning of the individual, (b) The income tax allows for progressive taxation on the amount of money make.Without income tax, personal and corporate profits would be out of control and unregulated. Demerit of income tax is the implementation of an income tax system is very complex, especially when trying to regulate the rich and the corporations. So complicated in fact that an entire industry exists to simply monitor and control the system.Some argue that for those in the lower middle class and lower classes, an earnings tax may be a financial hardship, regardless of the amount. In cases where households are just living by their means any deduction even the smallest may result in a significant decline in the standard of living, unlike income deductions to high grossing households who save the majority of their income.

Both payroll taxes and income taxes are based on an employee's wages or salary. The difference is who pays. A payroll tax is paid at least partly by the employer, while income taxes are paid by employees. Federal payroll taxes are for Social Security, Medicare and unemployment insurance. Withholding payroll and income taxes from employee wages is one part of being an employer.Psychologically, it seems as if all money taken out of a person's paycheck is the same, but income and payroll taxes serve very different functions, with contrasting effects.Many taxpayers may not even recognize the difference between the two levies, especially since both payroll and income taxes are withheld from their paychecks and the payroll tax is often listed on their pay stub

The basic difference is that wealth tax is charged on the wealth owned by a person. It would be pertinent to note that wealth doesn't include all assets but includes assets as defined in the wealth tax act. Whereas, income tax is charged on thc income earned by a person.Income tax is about what you earn and the government have papers with it so they can take tax from you about this income. Wealth tax is about what you have and it difference from country to another as how they saw the wealth money or number according to their people.Wealth is accumulated over time, i.e. the creation of wealth takes time. Income tax is charged on the income of an individual from various sources i.e. salary, house property, capital gains, business/ profession and other sources. As against this, wealth tax is levied on an individual or household's wealth.While income tax is payable on the income earned by individuals regularly, wealth tax is payable on the assets bought with the income after paying income tax.

• Wealth Tax

Wealth tax is charged under the Indian Wealth Tax Act, 1957 and the union government levies it. The tax is charged on individuals, Hindu Undivided Families (HUF) and companies in respect of the net wealth held by them during the assessment year. Indian citizens, resident companies and HUF are charged in respect of their worldwide assets, whereas non-resident is charged in respect of assets located in India. Among the assets subject to wealth tax there are, for example: buildings, or land belonging with them, used for residential or commercial purposes or as a guest house or farm house, within 25 km of the local limits or cantonment board; motor cars (other than those used in a business car-hire or which are stock-in-trade); jewels or precious metals (unless they are stock-in-trade); yachts, boats and aircraft (unless used for commercial purposes); urban land (with some exclusion); cash in hand in excess of Rs 50,000 (Bernardi & Fraschini, 2005).

• Other Taxes on Capital and Property

Other taxes on capital and property are levied by the states and the local authorities.

(a) The states impose: - a land tax on the value of land (the methods of valuation and the rates vary from states to states); - a tax on motor vehicles, whose yield is used for the development and the maintenance of state roads.

(b) The local authorities impose: - land cesses in the form of a surcharge on land revenue; - a tax on land and buildings, generally based on the annual rental value; - betterment taxes, based on increases of land value caused by town planning and town improvement; - taxes on the transfer of immovable property, based on the value of the property and in addition to state stamp duty (Bernardi & Fraschini, 2005).

• Expenditure Tax

The expenditure tax is charged under the Indian Expenditure-tax Act, 1987 and it is imposed by the union government. The tax is charged at the rate of 10 per cent on any chargeable expenditure incurred in a hotel wherein the room charges for any unit of residential accommodation are three thousand rupees or more per day. The expenditure tax is collected by the person who carries on the business of such hotel (Bernardi & Fraschini, 2005).

Advantages of Direct Tax

- Direct taxes are also in accordance with the canon of certainty, which is an important to consider. The canon of certainty states that the amount of tax should be certain and definite to the taxpayer.
- Direct tax is that it creates social awareness among the general public.
- Direct taxes is that they might be used as an anti-inflationary measure.
- A direct tax satisfies the canon of certainty. For instance, a person liable to pay income tax knows how much he will be required to pay; for that purpose, he can appropriate steps beforehand.
- Direct taxes constitute an important source of government revenue. Their collection charges are also low.
- A direct tax has elasticity. It can be varied according to the needs of the government and changes in the income of the people (Suman, 2017).

Disadvantages of Direct Tax

- Probably the biggest disadvantage of direct taxes is that it leads to tax evasion and corruption in a society.By submitting false returns, many people try to evade income tax.
- Another great disadvantage of the direct taxes is that they are usually not in accordance with the canon of convenience.
- Another disadvantage of direct taxes is that they reduce the desire to work and save. The rate of direct taxes are usually high.
- such taxes are not very popular, because the people have to bear the burden of such taxes directly (Suman, 2017).

Indirect Taxes

An indirect tax is a tax collected by an intermediary (such as a retail store) from the person who bears the ultimate economic burden of the tax (such as the consumer). An indirect tax may increase the price of goods to raise the price of the products for the consumers. Examples would be fuel, liquor, and cigarette taxes. Indirect taxation is policy commonly used to generate tax revenue. Indirect tax is so called as it is paid indirectly by the final consumer of goods and services while paying for purchase of goods or for enjoying services.

Types of Indirect Tax

• Customs Duties

The Constitution has given to the union the right to legislate and collect duties on goods imported into or exported from India. The Customs Act, 1962 is the basic Statute, effective from 1st February 1963. The categories of items and the rates of duties which are leviable have been specified in two schedules to the Customs Tariff Act, 1975. The custom duty on exports is levied on items listed in the second schedule to Customs Tariff Act, 1975. Currently, the rates vary from 10 to 60 per cent and they are either ad valorem, specific or a combination of both. Very few items are subject to customs duties on their export. Under the Custom Tariff Act, 1975 and other laws, there are the following types of duties that are leviable:

(a) Basic Customs Duty - that is duty specified against each heading or sub-heading in the first schedule. There are different rates of duty for different commodities and there are preferential rates for goods imported from certain countries in accordance with bilateral agreements with such countries. The duty may be ad valorem or specific.

(b) Surcharge - that is levied at the rate of 10 per cent of the Basic Customs Duty on imported goods, unless exempted by a notification.

(c) Additional duty of customs - equivalent to the excise duty leviable on goods produced or manufactured in India. Generally, it is on ad valorem basis, though specific rates are prescribed for some tems. For imported goods to be used as inputs for manufacture of other goods, it is generally eligible for a credit (called CENVAT credit) equal to the additional duty of customs paid on the imported goods. This credit can be used for paying central excise duties.

(d) Special additional duty – whose amount is computed by applying the specified rate on the total of the assessable value, the basic customs duty and the additional duty of customs described above (Bernardi & Fraschini, 2005).

- **Central Excise Duties**

Central excise duties are charged under the Central Excise Act, 1944 at the rates specified in the schedules to the Central Excise Tariff Act, 1985. They are an indirect tax levied on goods produced or manufactured in India, excluding those produced or manufactured in special economic zones. The duty is payable by the manufacturer at the time of removal of goods from the factory premises or warehouse; the taxable base is the wholesale price of the goods manufactured.

There are several types of duties which become payable at the time of clearance of such goods. These duties are:

(a) Basic excise duty (specified against each sub-heading in the First Schedule to the Central Excise Tariff Act, 1985) actually called the "Central Value Added Tax (CENVAT)

(b) Special excise duty (leviable only on a few items, in addition to CENVAT, at the rate specified under the Second Schedule to the Central Excise Tariff Act, 1985).

(c) Additional duties of excise (leviable on various commodities, as specified textiles and textile articles, or on sugar, tobacco products in lieu of sales tax).

(d) Cess (on different items - for example, spices, agriculture and processed food products, coffee, marine products which are exported - through special enactment) (Bernardi & Fraschini, 2005).

Merits of Excise Duty are: (a) Major source of Government revenue; (b) Psychological advantages to tax payer; (c) Easier to collect; (d) Balanced Industrial Growth; (e) Less collection cost; (f) Tax evasion difficult, and (g) Control over wasteful expenditure. Disadvantages or demerits of Excise Duty are (a) Increase the Price of goods; (b) The incidence is uniform; (c) Reduces demand of goods; and (d) Increases project costs.

- **Service Tax**

Service tax was introduced in India for the first time in 1994. It extends to whole of India except the state of Jammu and Kashmir. It is levied, collected and appropriated by the union government. Service tax is levied on specified taxable services and the responsibility of payment of the tax is cast on the service provider. Initially the service tax was imposed on the following services: telephone, stockbroker, general insurance. Over the years it was extended to other services, as advertising agencies and courier agencies. Service tax is levied on the gross or aggregate amount charged by the service provider on the receiver; only in particular cases the tax is permitted to be paid on the value received (Bernardi & Fraschini, 2005).

• Sales tax

Sales tax is charged under the Central Sales Tax Act, 1956. It is levied on the sale or purchase of goods. There are two kinds of sales tax: (1) central sales tax (CST), imposed by the union government; (2) sales tax, imposed by each state. Central sales tax is generally payable on the sale of all goods by a dealer in the course of inter-state trade and commerce and it is levied in the state where the movement of goods commences. Although the tax is imposed by the central government, the revenue is administered by the state in which it is levied. Sales tax on intra-state sale or purchase of goods (other than newspapers) may only be imposed by the state in which the sale or purchase takes place (Bernardi & Fraschini, 2005).

Advantages of Indirect Tax

Some of the merits or advantages of indirect tax are:

- It touches all income groups. Direct tax, like income tax, is imposed on persons having a certain minimum level of income.
- By imposing an indirect tax, the consumption of an undesir-able thing can be discouraged.
- People are not always conscious of indirect taxes because, in most cases, it is combined with the price.
- Indirect tax also enlarges the revenue receipts of the government. By the levy of indirect taxes, the tax net is cast wider and all people are made to contribute to the national fund.

Disadvantages of Indirect Tax

Some demerits of indirect tax are:

- The main draw-back of an indirect tax is that it is now an equitable tax. It is regressive in nature. It affects the poorer section more than the rich.
- Indirect taxes create various administrative problems.The collection of an indirect tax like customs duty often involves large expenses.

In Summary the merits and demerits of direct tax and indirect tax are

Tax	*Merit*	*Demerit*
Direct	1. Equitable in that it falls on those who can afford to pay. 2. Gives the government direct control over peoples spending.	1. Discourages hard work and enterprise 2. Increases the time and resources spend on tax avoidance. 3. The tax on company profits tends to reduce investment. 4. Can be difficult and costly to collect.
Indirect Tax	1. Does not discourage effort. 2. Can be used for specific social politics such as reducing smoking or gambling. 3. People have a degree of choice in whether they will pay the tax. 4. Relatively cheap and easy to collect.	1. Indirect taxes are regressive: as a proportion of income they fall more heavily on the poor. 2. The amount of revenue to be raised by excise duty or sales tax cannot easily be predicted.

Source:http://www.economicsdiscussion.net/taxes/indirect-taxes/merits-and-demerits-of-indirect-taxes/12794

Table 1.1: Difference between Direct Tax and Indirect Tax

Sl. No.	*Direct Tax*	*Indirect Tax*
1.	Direct tax is levied and paid for by individuals, Hindu undivided Families, firms, companies etc.	Indirect tax is ultimately paid for by the end-consumer of goods and services.
2.	The burden of tax cannot be shifted in case of direct taxes.	The burden of tax can be shifted for indirect taxes.
3.	Lack of administration in collection of direct taxes can make tax evasion possible.	Indirect taxes cannot be evaded as the taxes are charged on goods and services.
4.	Direct tax can help in reducing inflation.	Indirect tax may enhance inflation.
5.	Direct taxes have better allocative effects than indirect taxes as direct taxes put lesser burden over the collection of amount than indirect taxes.	Collection is scattered across parties and consumers' preferences of goods is distorted from the price variations due to indirect taxes.
6.	Direct taxes help in reducing inequalities and are considered to be progressive.	Indirect taxes enhance inequalities and are considered to be regressive.
7.	Direct taxes have many exemptions and involve higher administrative costs.	Indirect taxes involve lesser administrative costs due to convenient and stable collections.
8.	Direct reduce savings and discourage investments.	Indirect taxes are oriented more towards growth as they discourage consumption and help enhance savings.
9.	Direct taxes are collected only from people in respective tax brackets.	Indirect taxes have a wider coverage as all members of the society are taxed through the sale of goods and services.
10.	Income tax is charged on the personal income of a person.	Sales tax is paid on the sale of goods, product and any kind of services.
11.	Income tax can be avoided but it is hard to avoid the sales tax as it is wrapped in the price of product or service that is being purchased by the customer.	A customer will automatically pay the sales tax when he will purchase a specific product or service.
12	Income tax is a direct tax.	sales tax is an indirect tax.

Source: https://www.bankbazaar.com/tax/difference-between-direct-tax-and-indirect-tax.html

Table 1.2: Difference between Income Tax and Sales Tax

Sl. No.	*Income Tax*	*Sales Tax*
1.	Income tax is a direct tax paid by individuals on their income.	Sales tax is a pass-through tax charged on a sale
2.	Individuals pay federal income tax.	Sales tax is administered at a state level only, and consumers who live in states with a sales tax pay it to merchants at the point of sale.
3.	Essentially all income-earning individuals have to deal with income tax.	Only product sellers or people who sell certain services have to deal with collecting and remitting sales tax back to the state.

Source: https://blog.taxjar.com/difference-sales-tax-income-tax/

Table 1.3: Difference between Income Tax and Wealth Tax

Sl. No.	*Income Tax*	*Wealth Tax*
1.	Income refers to the money received or earned on a continuous basis, as a return for work or investments.	Wealth implies money or valuable possession accumulated by a person during the course of his life
2.	Flow of money.	Stock of assets.
3.	Income is generated immediately.	Wealth is created over time.

Source: https://keydifferences.com/difference-between-income-and-wealth.html

Table 1.4: Difference between Sales Tax and Excise Duty

Sl. No.	*Sales Tax*	*Excise Duty*
1.	A sales tax is a tax that is levied on the sale of certain goods and services. This tax is payable by the consumer, at the time of purchase.	An excise duty is also known as excise, excise tax, or even a duty of excise special tax. It is an inland tax on the sale, or production for sale, of specific goods within the country.
2.	Sales tax is usually a percentage of the total cost and is proportional to the price of the good.	Excise duty is typically a per unit tax.
3.	Sales tax is borne by the consume	Excise duty is also usually paid by the manufacturer.
4.	Sales tax is payable after the sale takes place.	Excise duty is payable on removal of goods from factory or warehouse
5.	Sales tax is charged on sale price.	Excise duty is levied on accessible value.

Source: http://www.differencebetween.info/difference-between-sales-tax-and-excise-duty

Table 1.5: Difference between Excise Duty and Custom Duty

Sl. No.	*Excise Duty*	*Custom Duty*
1.	The duty that is levied for goods manufactured inside the state is called excise duty.	The duty that is levied on goods imported from a foreign country is the customs duty.
2.	Excise duty is valued ad valoreum.	The customs duty of any goods is valued by its assessable value.

Source: https://www.differencebetween.com/difference-between-excise-duty-and-custom-duty/

Tax Reforms in India

Tax is the major source of revenue to government in India. Taxes are levied as per the laws prescribed in constitution of India. It is levied by central and state government and also by local bodies. The Development of any country's economy depends directly on the Country's Taxation Structure. A Taxation Structure which facilitates easy of doing business and having no chance for tax evasion brings prosperity to a country's economy. In India, the Taxes are classified in to two types, direct taxes and indirect taxes. Direct Taxes such as Corporation tax, Taxes on income, Estate duty, Interest Tax, Wealth Tax, Gift Tax, Land Revenue, Agricultural tax, Hotel receipts tax, Expenditure tax & Indirect Taxes such as Customs, Union excise duties, Service tax, State Excise duty, Stamp and registration fees, General Sales tax, Taxes on vehicle, Entertainment tax, Taxes on goods and passengers, Taxes and duties on electricity & Taxes on purchase of sugarcane (Shah & Joshi, 2017).

India has a tax structure with a three-tier federal structure (the union government, the state governments and the urban/rural local bodies). The main taxes/duties that the union government is empowered to levy are: income tax, customs duties, excise duties, sales tax and service tax. The main taxes levied by the state governments are sales tax, stamp duty, state excise, land revenue, duty on entertainment and tax on professions & callings. The local bodies are empowered to levy tax on properties, octroi, tax on markets and tax/user charges for utilities. The room of the direct taxation, both on individuals and companies, is very smaller. India is a federal republic (union and states) with a complex structure of local authorities.

In 1991, in reaction to a severe macroeconomic crisis involving high fiscal deficits, India carried out a series of economic reforms, among which a tax reform. The main proposals comprised: (a) the reduction in the rates of the most important taxes; (b) the enlargement of all taxes' bases; (c) the transformation of the taxes on domestic production into something similar to a value added tax; (d) the simplification of laws and administrative procedures. In September 2002 the Government set up a new Task Force on tax reforms headed by V. Kelkar. The Kelkar committees suggested sweeping reforms including: (a) raising the limits of income tax exemption and two-tier brackets; b) cut in corporate tax rate; (c) three-rate basic customs duty structure; (d) service tax levied in a comprehensive manner; (e) repeal of wealth tax; (f) removal of tax exemptions, rationalization of incentives for savings and simplification of procedures; (g) gradual moving over the destination based, consumption type value added taxes at the state level (Bernardi & Fraschini, 2005).

According Rao (2000), one of the most important reasons for recent tax reforms in many developing and transitional economies has been to evolve a tax system to meet the requirements of international competition. The transition from a public sector based, heavy industry dominated, import substituting industrialization strategy to one of allocating resources according to market signals has necessitated systemic changes in the tax system. From the 1970s to mid-1980s in India, there has been a steady increase in the tax-GDP ratio in keeping with the buoyant economic conditions and acceleration in the growth rate of the economy. The economic recession following the severe drought of 1987 resulted in stagnation in revenues in the second phase until 1992-93. Following the economic crisis of 1991 and the subsequent reforms in the tax system, particularly reduction in tariffs, actually caused a decline in the tax ratio.

There have been a number of attempts at improving the tax system since independence. The principal objective of these attempts has been to enhance revenue productivity to finance large development plans. The first comprehensive attempt at reforming the tax system was by the Tax Reform Committee in 1953. Since then, there have been a number of attempts, most of them partial, to remedy various aspects of the tax system. The expenditure tax levied on the recommendation of the Kaldor Committee in 1957-58 had to be withdrawn after three years as it did not generate the expected revenues. The consequent moral hazard problems led the Direct Taxes Enquiry Committee in 1971 to recommend a significant reduction in marginal tax rates. On the indirect taxes side, a major simplification exercise was attempted by the Indirect Taxes Enquiry Committee in 1972. On the indirect taxes front, the most important reform before 1991 was the conversion of the union excise duties into a modified value added tax (MODVAT) in 1986. The MODVAT was introduced in a limited manner on a few commodities and the coverage was gradually extended over the years. It was an income type VAT applicable only to a few manufactured goods.

Tax reform since 1991 was initiated as a part of the structural reform process, following the economic crisis of 1991. The government accepted the recommendations of the TRC and has implemented them in phases. Although it did not entirely follow the recommendations and is yet to implement many of the measures to strengthen the administration and enforcement machinery, most of the recommendations have been implemented. Voluntary disclosure scheme to allow a one-time amnesty to tax defaulters by paying the necessary tax was introduced in 1997-98. Besides reduction in the number of rates, the tax has been progressively converted from a specific into ad valorem levy in respect of the majority of commodities. The facility of providing credit on input taxes under the MODVAT too has been progressively extended to a larger number of commodities.

Table 1.6: Reforms in Indirect Taxation System Year

Reforms in Indirect Taxation System Year	*Reforms*
1974	Report of LK Jha Committee suggested VAT should be introduced
1986	Introduction of a restricted VAT called MODVAT
1991	Report by the Chelliah Committee recommended either VAT or GST which was accepted by Government
1994	Introduction of Service Tax @ 5%
1999	Formation of Empowered Committee on State VAT
2000	Implementation of uniform floor rate of tax for VAT at the rate 1%, 4% and 12.5%. and Abolition of tax related incentives granted by States
2003	VAT implemented in Haryana in April 2003
2004	Significant progress towards CENVAT, MODVAT was abolished and credit account was merged with service tax and excise to provide for cross utilization.
2005-06	VAT implemented in 26 more states
2007	First GST released by Mr. P. Shome in January. Finance Minister announces for GST in budget Speech and CST phase out starts in April 2007. Then, Joint Working Group formed and submitted report
2008	EC finalizes the view on GST structure in April 2008
2009	First discussion paper on GST was released and commission submitted report proposing GST to be implemented from 1.4.2010
2010	Department of Revenue commented on GST discussion paper and Finance Minister suggested probable GST rate.
2011	Team was set up to lay down road map for GST and 115th Constitutional Amendment Bill for GST was laid down in Parliament
2012	Negative list regime for service tax was implemented
2013	Parliamentary Standing Committee submitted its report on the Bill
2014	115th Amendment Bill lapsed and was reintroduced in 122nd Constitutional Amendment Bill
2017	Implementation of GST from July 1, 2017.

Source: Akanksha Khurana, Aastha Sharma, (2016)

Another important change that has been brought about since 1991 is the introduction of a selective tax on services. The constitution does not assign this tax base specifically either to the centre or the states. With the assistance of the Canadian International Development Agency (CIDA), the government has started an ambitious programme of computerising tax returns and building a management information system (Rao, 2000). With its new GST, India joins some 160 countries globally in imposing a form of value added tax (VAT). These taxes are widely acknowledged as progressive, with inbuilt efficiencies to broaden the tax base, decrease the cascading effect of multiple indirect taxes and contain revenue leakage.

Table1.7: Major Taxes Being Levied in the Supply Chain of Goods by the State/Central Government

Sl. No.	*Taxes*	*Taxable Event*	Nature of Tax
1.	State VAT	Sale of Goods within the State	State Tax
2.	Excise Duty	Manufacturing of Goods	Central Tax
3.	Central Sales tax	Sale of Goods between two States	State Tax
4.	Additional Customs Duty	Import of Goods	Central Tax
5.	Special Additional Duty	Import of Goods	Central Tax
6.	Entry Tax	Entry of Goods in to Local Area	State Tax

Source: https://www.taxmann.com/blogpost/2000000038/types-of-gst-in-india.aspx

Seen as one of the biggest tax reforms (in terms of indirect taxes) since 1947, GST is set to bring forth unprecedented transformation of the country from a political union to an economic union of 29 states and 7 union territories. Under this fabled tax system, existing in developed countries such as France, U.K. and Canada, the tax payers in India will pay a consolidated tax instead of the plethora of taxes such as Value-Added Tax, Central Excise, Service Tax, Entry Tax or Octroi, Customs Duty, Central Surcharge & Cess, Luxury Tax, Entertainment Tax, and Purchase Tax and a few other indirect taxes. Thereby helping to consolidate, streamline and make easier and more effective the process of indirect taxation.

India's GST replace a complex web of existing taxes, bringing uniform tax rates and rules and simplifying compliance for businesses. The list of taxes subsumed by the proposed GST is expected to spell the end for most existing central and state taxes on supplies of goods and services, including central excise and service tax, central sales tax, state VATs and other local levies on goods. India operate a dual GST. The central and state governments will levy the GST on supplies of both goods and services on a common taxable value and receive the revenues from their component of the tax. Imports and interstate supplies will attract an Integrated GST (IGST) levied by central government.

Bouncy and Elasticity of a Tax

Tax buoyancy is an indicator to measure efficiency and responsiveness of revenue mobilization in response to growth in the Gross domestic product or National income. A tax is said to be buoyant if the tax revenues increase more than proportionately in response to a rise in national income or output. A tax is buoyant when revenues increase by more than, say, 1 per cent for a 1 per cent increase in GDP. Tax buoyancy explains this relationship between the changes in government's tax revenue growth and the changes in GDP. Usually, tax elasticity is considered a better indicator to measure tax responsiveness.

Impact of Tax

The incidence of taxation refers to this question of who and in what proportion bears the final burden of a tax. It is not necessary that a person or a firm who pays a tax to the Government or, in other words, bears the initial burden of a tax will also be one on whom the final burden of the tax rests. This is because a tax can be shifted or transferred to others. Therefore, in economics, we distinguish between the impact and incidence of a tax.

Incidence of Tax

The incidence of taxation refers to this question of who and in what proportion bears the final burden of a tax. It is not necessary that a person or a firm who pays a tax to the Government or, in other words, bears the initial burden of a tax will also be one on whom the final burden of the tax rests. This is because a tax can be shifted or transferred to others. Therefore, in economics, we distinguish between the impact and incidence of a tax.

Shifting of Tax

Incidence is final resting place of a tax while shifting is process of transferring money burden of tax to someone else. Shifting finally ends in incidence. When a person on whom tax is levied tries to shift tax on to the other, he may succeed in shifting tax completely, partly, or may not succeed at all. Shifting of tax can take place in two directions, forward and backward. If tax is shifted, from seller to consumer, it is a case of forwarding shifting. Backward shifting takes place when consumers do not purchase commodities at increased prices. Sellers are then forced to cut down prices and bear burden of tax themselves. Backward shifting is thus performed by buyers.

Value Added Tax Reform

The major landmark in coordinated tax reform at the state level was the simplification and rationalization of the sales tax system, beginning in

1999 and the introduction of a value added tax in twenty-one states on April 1, 2005, to replace the existing cascading sales tax.Considerations of fiscal autonomy and demands on the central government to effect sizable interregional resource transfers as well as the political acceptability tilted the decision in favour of the dual VAT scheme as a medium-term goal. In the medium term, as part of the initiative to introduce a dual VAT, it has been decided to convert the cascading state-level sales taxes into a destination-based VAT.

To persuade the states to rationalize their tax systems along the lines recommended by the study group, the government of India appointed a State Finance Ministers' Committee to make recommendations to phase in the VAT within a given time frame. The committee, which was subsequently transformed into the Empowered Committee of State Finance Ministers, recommended that the states adopt floor rates to minimize the "race to the bottom." The committee's recommendation that the VAT be implemented in 2003 was postponed repeatedly, until April 2005. It was implemented in 2005.

The salient features of the April 2005 reform are summarized here:

- The tax is levied at two rates (except for bullion, specie, and precious metals, which are taxed at 1 per cent). Basic necessities (about 75 items) are exempted. Most items of common consumption, inputs,and capital goods (about 275 items) are taxed at 4 per cent, and all other items are taxed at 12.5 per cent. Gasoline and diesel fuel (which contribute about 40 per cent of the sales tax) are kept outside the VAT regime, and a floor rate of 20 per cent is to be levied on them.
- The tax credit facility covers inputs and purchases as well as capital goods for both manufacturers and dealers. Credit for taxes paid on capital goods can be used over three years of sales.
- The tax credit mechanism operates fully only for intrastate sales. In interstate transactions, the exporting state is supposed to give an input tax credit for purchases made locally, against the collection of the central sales tax. The central sales tax credit in the importing state, or other mechanisms of zero-rating of interstate sales, will be introduced in two years, when the central sales tax in its present form will be phased out. In the meantime, an information system on interstate trade will be built up.
- The central government has agreed to compensate the states for any loss of revenue at rates of 100 per cent in the first year,

75 per cent in the second year, and 50 per cent in the third year. The loss will be calculated by estimating the difference between the projected sales tax revenue using 2004–05 as the base and the actual revenue collected. The projected revenues will be estimated by applying the average of the best three years' growth rates during the last five years.

- Tax incentives given to new industries by different states could be continued so long as it does not break the VAT chain. Many states propose to convert tax holidays into deferment of the tax.
- All dealers with annual turnover above Rs 500,000 are required to register for the VAT. However, the states may levy a simple turnover tax not exceeding two per cent on those dealers with turnover up to Rs 5 million. Such dealers, paying the turnover tax, do not have to keep detailed accounts of their transactions. But these small dealers will not be a part of the VAT chain, and no credit will be available for the taxes paid on purchases from these dealers. They may therefore voluntarily register as regular VAT dealers (Rao & Rao, 2006).

Chapter - 2

Value Added Tax

Value-added tax is a type of general consumption tax that is collected incrementally, based on the increase in value of a product or service at each stage of production or distribution. It is usually implemented as a destination-based tax, where the tax rate is based on the location of the customer.It is a form of sales tax collected at each point of sale of goods in the production and distribution chain with a provision to set off or credit the tax paid on purchase of such goods against the tax payable on its sales. Thus, tax is essentially collected, on the value addition at each point of such sale. VAT is payable, when there is sale of taxable goods; (a) by a registered dealer assigned with TIN, (b) within the State, and (c) in course of business of the dealer.

Meaning and Concept

As the Wall Street Journal puts it, the VAT tax is "baked into the retail price." All European Union countries and many other countries around the world have a VAT or GST. The EU describes a VAT as: "a general tax that applies, in principle, to all commercial activities involving the production and distribution of goods and the provision of services. a consumption tax because it is borne ultimately by the final consumer. It is not a charge on businesses."

It is an indirect tax on the domestic consumption of goods and services, except those that are zero-rated (such as food and essential drugs) or are otherwise exempt (such as exports). It is levied at each stage in the chain of production and distribution from raw materials to the final sale based on the value (price) added at each stage. It is not a cost to the producer or the distribution chain members, and whereas its full brunt is borne by the end consumer, it avoids the double taxation (tax on tax) of a direct sales tax. VAT is tolerated by final consumers, so it is a consumption tax. Companies do not take the burden of VAT. Through a system of deductions, it is claimed fractionally, where taxable persons can abstract the VAT liability amount which they paid to other taxable persons on business activities purchase.

There are two main methods of calculating VAT: the credit-invoice or invoice-based method, and the subtraction or accounts-based method. Using the credit-invoice method, sales transactions are taxed, with the customer informed of the VAT on the transaction, and businesses may receive a credit for VAT paid on input materials and services. Using the subtraction method, at the end of a reporting period, a business calculates the value of all taxable sales then subtracts the sum of all taxable purchases and the VAT rate is applied to the difference.

Germany and France were the first countries to implement VAT, doing so in the form of a general consumption tax during World War I. The modern variation of VAT was first implemented by France in the 1950s. The amount of VAT is decided by the state as per centage of the end-market price. As its name suggests, value-added tax is designed to tax only the value added by a business on top of the services and goods it can purchase from the market. The value-added effect is achieved by prohibiting end-consumers from recovering VAT on purchases, but permitting businesses to do so. The VAT collected by the state is computed as the difference between the VAT of sales earnings and the VAT of those goods and services upon which the product depends.

Value-added tax avoids the cascade effect of sales tax by taxing only the value added at each stage of production. For this reason, throughout the world, VAT has been gaining favour over traditional sales taxes. In principle, VAT applies to all provisions of goods and services. The VAT mechanism means that the end-user tax is the same as it would be with a sales tax. The main disadvantage of VAT is the extra accounting required by those in the middle of the supply chain; this is balanced by the simplicity of not requiring a set of rules to determine who is and is not considered an end user (Value added tax, 2018).More than 160 countries around the world use value-added taxation; it is most common in the European Union. But it is not without controversy.

Objectives of Value Added Tax

The objective for introducing VAT are:

- To avail credit on inputs leading to cost efficiency.
- Ensure equitable distribution of tax impact among dealers.
- Easy compliance through transparent and easy procedures exist under it and only two rates are there.
- Easy computation of tax.
- Avoids double taxation through input rebate.
- Prevents distortions in trade and economy through uniform tax rates.
- Calculation Easy and Simple
- Transparency
- Increased Tax Base
- Competitive Price

Difference between VAT and Turnover Tax

Value added tax differs from turnover tax as the turn over tax is imposed on the total value at each while VAT is imposed only on value added at that stage. VAT varies from sales tax in the sense that VAT is imposed at each stage of production and distribution whereas retail sales tax is imposed only at one stage, the final stage. It helps to minimize many problems related with tax evasion. Therefore, value added tax is more productive and less destructive than retail sales tax.

Features of Value Added Tax

The main characteristics of value added tax are stated as follows:

- VAT is a form of indirect taxation.
- VAT is a broad-based tax as it covers the value added to each commodity by a firm during all stages of production and distribution.
- VAT is based on value added principle. Value added can be obtained either by adding payments to factors of production or deducting cost of inputs from sales revenue.
- VAT is a substitute for sales tax, hotel tax. contract tax and entertainment tax.
- VAT is based on sclf-assessment system and provides the facility of tax credit and tax refund,

- VAT avoids cascading effect existed in sales tax and contains catch-up effect.

Types of Value Added Tax

The types of VAT are determined on the basis of treatment of capital goods of a firm. Input tax paid for capital goods is allowed or not is the fundamental question in the study of types of VAT. There are three types of VAT, they are:

- Consumption Type VAT: Under consumption type VAT, all capital goods purchased from other firms, in the year of purchase, are excluded from the tax base while depreciation is not deducted from the tax base in subsequent years. The base of tax is consumption since investment is relieved from taxation under this type.
- Income Type VAT: The income type VAT does not exclude capital goods purchased from other firms from the tax base in the year of purchase. This type, however, excludes depreciation from the tax base in subsequent years. The tax falls both on consumption and net investment. The tax base of this type is the net national income.
- GNP Type VAT: Under this type, capital goods purchased by a firm from other firms are not deductible from the tax base in the year of purchase. It also does not allow the deduction of depreciation from the tax base in subsequent years. Tax is levied both on consumption and gross investment. The tax base of this type is gross domestic product.

Principles Governing Value Added Tax

The following are the principles which govern value added tax:

- Principle of Transparency: VAT is transparent tax. It is an account based tax system. VAT has made tax system transparent.
- Principle of Removing Cascading Effect: VAT removes cascading effect. Cascading effect means tax on tax i.e. tax is charged on the value including tax. But VAT has removed this effect by not including the VAT in the cost price to the second stage of the distribution channel.
- Principle of Neutrality: Neutrality means not to discriminate one to another. VAT does not discriminate one economic activity against others.

- Principle of Destination and Zero Rating: Under this principle, goods and services are taxed at consumption point, bot based on production. Goods and services that are exported are taxed at zero rate.

Advantages of Value Added Tax

Following are the advantages of VAT:

- As compared to other taxes, there is a less chance of tax evasion. VAT minimizes tax evasion due to its catch-up effect.
- VAT is simple to administer as compared to other indirect tax.
- VAT is transparent and has minimum burden to consumers as it is collected in small fragments at various stages of production and distribution.
- VAT is based on value added not on total price. So, price does not increase as a result of VAT.
- There is mass participation of taxpayers.

Disadvantages of Value Added Tax

Following are the disadvantages of VAT:

- VAT is costly to implement as it is based on full billing system.
- VAT is relatively complex to understand. The calculation of value added in every stage is not an easy task.
- To implement the VAT successfully, customers, need to be conscious, otherwise tax evasion will be widespread.

Chapter - 3

Goods and Services Tax

The income of the government through all sources is called public income or public revenue. In its wider sense it includes all the incomes or receipts which a public authority may secure during any period of time. As such, receipts from public borrowings (or public debt) and from the sale of public assets are mainly excluded from public revenue.A fund raised through the various taxes is referred to as tax revenue. Taxes are compulsory contributions imposed by the government on its citizens to meet its general expenses incurred for the common good, without any corresponding benefits to the tax payer.

Taxes constitute a significant part of public revenue in modern public finance. Taxes have macro-economic effects. Taxation can affect the size and mode of consumption, pattern of production and distribution of income and wealth. Progressive taxes can help in reducing inequalities of income and wealth by lowering the high income group's disposable income.Public income received through the administration, commercial enterprises, gifts and grants are the source of non-tax revenues of the government.

Profits of state undertakings are an important source of revenue these days, owing to the expansion of the public sector.In modern times, grants from one government to another have a greater importance. Local governments receive grants from state governments and state governments from the centre. The central government gives grants- in-aid to state governments in order to enable them to carry out their functions

What is Goods and Services Tax?

Goods and Services Tax (GST) is most ambitious and biggest tax reform plan, which aims to stitch together a common market by dismantling fiscal barriers between states. It is an indirect tax levied in India on the sale of goods and services. It is a single national uniform tax levied across India on all goods and services. In GST, all the indirect taxes will be subsumed under a single regime. The GST taxation laws will put an end to multiple taxes which are levied on different products, starting from the source of manufacturing to reaching the end consumer. It works on the fundamental Principle of "One Country One Tax".

The tax compliance is going to be easy as all the laws are subsumed and only one GST law to be implemented. The four GST slabs have been set at 5 per cent, 12 per cent, 18 per cent and 28 per cent for different items or services. The integration of tax laws in GST is expected to reduce the tax burden on the tax payer compared to present system where the tax payer's burden is high. Presently the tax is at two points i.e., when the product moves out of factory and other at the retail outlet (Rupa, 2017).GST is a destination based tax which is levied only on value addition at each stage because credits of input taxes paid at procurement of inputs will be available. Thus, the final consumer will bear only the GST charged by the last dealer in the supply chain, with set-off benefits at all the previous stages (Kashyap, 2017).

On 30 June 2017, during a special parliament assembly at night, Indian Prime Minister Narendra Modi addressed the nation and launched the Goods and Services Tax in the central hall, where first Prime Minister of independent India Jawaharlal Nehru delivered his famous 'tryst with destiny' speech on 15 August, 1947 ((Kashyap, 2017). The tax came into effect from July 1, 2017 through the implementation of One Hundred and First Amendment of the Constitution of India by the Modi government. The tax replaced existing multiple cascading taxes levied by the central and state governments. The tax rates, rules and regulations are governed by the Goods and Services Tax Council which comprises finance ministers of centre and all the states. GST simplified a slew of indirect taxes with a unified tax.

GST will be payable at the final point of consumption on the price of goods and services; termed as a "transaction value." This transaction value or actual paid price, while buying the good or service, will include packing cost, commission, and all other expenses incurred for their sales. To start with, the GST Council has finalized four tax rates slabs of 5 per cent, 12 per cent, 18 per cent and 28 per cent for goods and services. Education, healthcare, milk products and alcohol will continue to be exempted from tax in the upcoming GST regime. Similarly, gold and rough diamonds do not fall under the current rate slabs and will be taxed at 3 per cent and 0.25 per cent respectively (Kashyap, 2017).

Global Perspectives of GST

Several countries have already established the Goods and Services Tax. In Australia, the system was introduced in 2000 to replace the Federal Wholesale Tax. GST was implemented in New Zealand in 1986. A hidden Manufacturer's Sales Tax was replaced by GST in Canada, in the year 1991. In Singapore, GST was implemented in 1994. GST is a value-added tax in Malaysia that came into effect in 2015.

History of Goods and Service Tax

According Nihar (2017), although, it was in 2000 that Vajpayee Government set up an Empowered Committee to discuss GST, the idea however, concerning its implementation was first announced by the then Union Finance Minister, Shri P. Chidambaram in the Central Budget (2007-2008). The announcement led to further detailed discussions on the report by the Empowered Committee of State Finance Ministers that was set up as a Joint Working Group on May 10, 2007.The First Discussion Paper by the Empowered Committee on Goods and Service Tax was released on November 10th, 2009.

The Constitution provided for Centre to tax the services and goods up till the production stage and for State to tax the sale of goods. However, the Centre and the State did not have the power to levy tax on 'supply of goods and services'. Hence, the 115th Amendment Bill was tabled before the Parliament on March 22, 2011 to give concurrent taxing powers to both the Union and the State. With the introduction of 122nd Constitution Amendment Bill, the former was replaced. It received assent from the President, Pranab Mukherjee on September 8, 2016. In summary we can show the trends as shown in website of bankbazaar.

- **2000:** In India, the idea of adopting GST was first suggested by the Atal Bihari Vajpayee Government in 2000. The state finance ministers formed an Empowered Committee (EC) to create a structure for GST, based on their experience in designing State VAT. Representatives from the Centre and states were requested to examine various aspects of the GST proposal and create reports on the thresholds, exemptions, taxation of inter-state supplies, and taxation of services. The committee was headed by Asim Dasgupta, the finance minister of West Bengal. Dasgupta chaired the committee till 2011.

- 2004: A task force that was headed by Vijay L. Kelkar the advisor to the finance ministry, indicated that the existing tax structure had many issues that would be mitigated by the GST system.
- February 2005: The finance minister, P. Chidambaram, said that the medium-to-long term goal of the government was to implement a uniform GST structure across the country, covering the whole production-distribution chain. This was discussed in the budget session for the financial year 2005-06.
- February 2006: The finance minister set 1 April 2010 as the GST introduction date.
- November 2006: Parthasarthy Shome, the advisor to P. Chidambaram, mentioned that states will have to prepare and make reforms for the upcoming GST regime.
- February 2007: The 1 April 2010 deadline for GST implementation was retained in the union budget for 2007-08.
- February 2008: At the union budget session for 2008-09, the finance minister confirmed that considerable progress was being made in the preparation of the roadmap for GST. The targeted timeline for the implementation was confirmed to be 1 April, 2010.
- July 2009: Pranab Mukherjee, the new finance minister of India, announced the basic skeleton of the GST system. The 1 April 2010 deadline was being followed then as well.
- November 2009: The EC that was headed by Asim Dasgupta put forth the First Discussion Paper (FDP), describing the proposed GST regime. The paper was expected to start a debate that would generate further inputs from stakeholders.
- February 2010: The government introduced the mission-mode project that laid the foundation for GST. This project, with a budgetary outlay of Rs 1,133 crores, computerised commercial taxes in states. Following this, the implementation of GST was pushed by one year.
- March 2011: The government led by the Congress party puts forth the Constitution (115th Amendment) Bill for the introduction of GST. Following protest by the opposition party, the Bill was sent to a standing committee for a detailed examination.

- June 2012: The standing committee starts discussion on the Bill. Opposition parties raise concerns over the 279B clause that offers additional powers to the Centre over the GST dispute authority.
- November 2012: P. Chidambaram and the finance ministers of states hold meetings and set the deadline for resolution of issues as 31 December, 2012.
- February 2013: The finance minister, during the budget session, announces that the government will provide Rs 9,000 crore as compensation to states. He also appeals to the state finance ministers to work in association with the government for the implementation of the indirect tax reform.
- August 2013: The report created by the standing committee is submitted to the parliament. The panel approves the regulation with few amendments to the provisions for the tax structure and the mechanism of resolution.
- October 2013: The state of Gujarat opposes the Bill, as it would have to bear a loss of Rs 14,000 crore per annum, owing to the destination-based taxation rule.
- May 2014: The Constitution Amendment Bill lapses. This is the same year that Narendra Modi was voted into power at the Centre.
- December 2014: India's new finance minister, Arun Jaitley, submits the Constitution (122nd Amendment) Bill, 2014 in the parliament. The opposition demanded that the Bill be sent for discussion to the standing committee.
- February 2015: Jaitley, in his budget speech, indicated that the government is looking to implement the GST system by 1 April, 2016.
- May 2015: The Lok Sabha passes the Constitution Amendment Bill. Jaitley also announced that petroleum would be kept out of the ambit of GST for the time being.
- August 2015: The Bill is not passed in the Rajya Sabha. Jaitley mentions that the disruption had no specific cause.
- March 2016: Jaitley says that he is in agreement with the Congress's demand for the GST rate not to be set above 18 per cent. But he is not inclined to fix the rate at 18 per cent. In the future if the Government, in an unforeseen emergency, is required to raise the tax rate, it would have to take the permission of the parliament. So, a fixed rate of tax is ruled out.

- June 2016: The Ministry of Finance releases the draft model law on GST to the public, expecting suggestions and views.
- August 2016: The Congress-led opposition finally agrees to the Government's proposal on the four broad amendments to the Bill. The Bill was passed in the Rajya Sabha.
- September 2016: The Honourable President of India gives his consent for the Constitution Amendment Bill to become an Act.
- 2017: Four Bills related to GST become Act, following approval in the parliament and the President's assent: Central GST Bill, Integrated GST Bill, Union Territory GST Bill, and GST (Compensation to States) Bill.

(**Source:** https://www.bankbazaar.com/tax/history-of-gst.html)

Types of GST in India

There would be three different types of levies in GST:

- CGST
- SGST/UTGST
- IGST

Table 3.1: Wider Implications of GST

Suppliers	End of old system e.g. sales tax exemption Preferential GST vendors-maximise tax credits Use of self-billing / other billing best practices to maximise tax credits
Customers	Pricing modelling Structure of offers / financing
Finance & Administration	Impact on cash flow Identification of transaction and GST liability Maximisation of GST tax credit on purchases Registration & compliance Cancellation of licences –potential audit?
Internal / Human Capital	Training and communication
Legal	GST impact on contracts Current contracts Future contracts
Strategy	GST impact on corporate plans e.g. restructuring, new projects and transactions Clarification of issues and treatment with tax review panel Availing advantage of Trade Facilitation Arrangements
Sales & Marketing Strategies	Effect on demand Pricing strategies Impact on current pipeline and inventory
Information Systems	Changes to Master and Transaction records Systems design changes for VAT / GST compliance

Source: https://www2.deloitte.com/in/en/pages/tax/articles/goods-and-services-tax.html

SGST would be leviable along with CGST on the supply made by a registered person within a State. Just as SGST is leviable along with CGST on the supply made by registered person within a State, UTGST would be levied along with CGST on the supply made by a registered person within a Union Territory. However, in no case, both SGST and UTGST would be leviable on an invoice of supply of goods or services or both. It would either be SGST or UTGST along with CGST would be leviable on the invoice. IGST would be leviable on Import or Inter-State supply of goods or services or both. IGST would be equivalent to sum total of CGST and SGST/UTGST.

Models of GST

Goods & Services Tax Law in India is a comprehensive, multi-stage, destination-based tax that is levied on every value addition. In simple words, Goods and Service Tax is an indirect tax levied on the supply of goods and services. This law has replaced many indirect tax laws that previously existed in India. It is one indirect tax for the entire country. Under the GST regime, the tax will be levied at every point of sale. In case of interstate sales, Central GST and State GST will be charged. Intra-state sales will be chargeable to Integrated GST.

- For Intra State Transactions: In case of Intra State transactions, Seller collects both CGST & SGST from the buyer and CGST needs to be deposited with Central Govt. and SGST with State Govt.
- For Inter State Transactions: Integrated Goods and Service Tax shall be levied on Inter State transactions of goods and services which are based on destination principle. Tax gets transferred to Importing state. Moreover, it is proposed to levy an additional tax on supply of goods, not exceeding one per cent, in the course of inter-state trade or commerce, to be collected by the Central Government for a period of two years, and assign to the States where the supply originates. Exports and Supplies to SEZ units will be zero rated (Rupa, 2017).

Objectives of GST

GST is proposed to perform the following objectives:

- GST would help to remove the cascading effects of production and distribution cost of goods and services. This would help to increase GDP and then to economic condition of the country.

- GST would remove the multiplicity of indirect taxation and reorganize all the indirect taxes which would be beneficial for manufacture and ultimate consumer.
- GST would be able to cover all the shortcomings of active VAT system and hopefully serve the economy health.
- Incidence of tax falls on household consumption
- The efficiency and equity of system is optimized
- There should be no export of taxes across taxing jurisdiction
- The Indian market should be integrated into single common market
- It enhances the cause of co-operative federalism (Shah & Joshi, 2017).

Taxes Subsumed into GST

Goods and Services Tax is the biggest indirect tax reform of India. It will subsume Central Excise Law, Service Tax Law, State VATs, Entry Tax, Luxury Taxes, Octroi etc. Earlier, there were so many taxes which were levied on goods such as Excise, VAR, entry tax, octroi. Similarly, service tax, entertainment tax, luxury tax were levied on services. Now, there will be only single tax i.e. GST and it will make dream of One Nation, One Tax feasible.

(a) Central Indirect Taxes

- Following Central Indirect Taxes and Levies would be subsumed in GST:
- Central Excise Duty
- Additional Excise Duties
- Excise Duty levied under the Medicinal and Toilet Preparations (Excise Duties) Act, 1955
- Service Tax
- Additional Customs Duty commonly known as Countervailing Duty
- Special Additional Duty of Customs
- Central Surcharges and Cess, so far as they relate to the supply of goods and services.

(b) State Indirect Taxes

Following State Indirect Taxes and Levies would be subsumed in GST:

- State Value Added Tax/Sales Tax

- Entertainment Tax (other than the tax levied by the local bodies)
- Central Sales Tax (levied by the Centre and collected by the States)
- Octroi and Entry Tax
- Purchase Tax
- Luxury Tax
- Taxes on lottery
- Betting and gambling
- State cess and surcharges insofar as they relate to supply of goods and services.

(**Source:** https://www.taxmann.com/blogpost/2000000039/what-are-the-central-state-indirect-taxes-and-levies-which-would-be-merged-in-gst.aspx)

Administration of GST in India

As per federal structure of India, there will be two components of GST – Central GST (CGST) and State GST (SGST). Both Centre and States will simultaneously levy GST across the value chain. Tax will be levied on every supply of goods and services. Centre would levy and collect Central Goods and Services Tax (CGST), and States would levy and collect the State Goods and Services Tax (SGST) on all transactions within a State. The input tax credit of CGST would be available for discharging the CGST liability on the output at each stage. Similarly, the credit of SGST paid on inputs would be allowed for paying the SGST on output. No cross utilization of credit would be permitted (Source: https://www.gstindia.com/about/).

Advantages of GST

GST mainly remove the Cascading effect on the sale of goods and services. Removal of cascading effect directly impact the cost of goods. Since tax on tax is eliminated in this regime, the cost of goods decreases. GST is also mainly technologically driven. All activities like registration, return filing, application for refund and response to notice needs to be done online on the GST Portal. This will speed up the processes. Other advantages are:

- GST is structured to simplify the current indirect system by removing multiple taxes. It creates India as a single market.
- A system of seamless tax-credits throughout the value-chain, and across boundaries of States, would ensure that there is minimal cascading of taxes.

- It taxes goods and services at the same rates so many disputes are eliminated on tax matter.
- Reduction in transaction costs of doing business would eventually lead to an improved competitiveness for the trade and industry.
- GST will be levied only at the final destination of consumption based on VAT principle and not at various points (from manufacturing to retail outlets). This will help in removing economic distortions and bring about development of a common national market.
- The subsuming of major Central and State taxes in GST, complete and comprehensive set-off of input goods and services and phasing out of Central Sales Tax would reduce the cost of locally manufactured goods and services.
- This will increase the competitiveness of Indian goods and services in the international market and give boost to Indian exports. The uniformity in tax rates and procedures across the country will also go a long way in reducing the compliance cost.
- The procedural cost is reduced due to uniform accounting namely, CGST, SGST, IGST have to be maintained for all types of taxes.
- The reduced tax burden on companies will reduce production cost making exporters more competitive at national and international level.
- More business entities including unorganized will come under the tax system thus widening the tax base. This may lead to better and more tax revenue collections.
- GST would make doing business in the country tax neutral, irrespective of the choice of place of doing business.
- Because of efficiency gains and prevention of leakages, the overall tax burden on most commodities will come down, which will benefit consumers.
- GST is expected to decrease the cost of collection of tax revenues of the Government, and will therefore, lead to higher revenue efficiency.
- Under GST, there would be only one tax from the manufacturer to the consumer, leading to transparency of taxes paid to the final consumer.
- Since all indirect taxes charged by the state governments and the central government will be subsumed by GST, it will become

simpler to administer the taxation system, especially because of the presence of a robust IT system.

- The cost of collecting taxes will decrease significantly with the implementation of GST, thereby resulting in higher revenue efficiency.
- A good number of products and/or services are either exempt from tax or charged at 5 per cent or less under GST, thereby making daily necessities more easily available to the poor.
- The average tax burden on industry and trade is expected to lower because of GST, resulting in a reduction of prices and increased consumption, which will eventually increase production and ultimately enhance the development of various industries.
- Certain sectors in the country, such as textile and construction, are highly unorganised and unregulated. GST aims to ensure that payments and compliances are done online, and input credit can only be availed when the supplier accepts the amount, thus ensuring that these industries have regulation and accountability.
- Since GST operate on an advanced IT platform, all GST-related issues will be addressed online, thereby ensuring ease and transparency in GST payments.
- Many businesses create depots and go downs in different states simply because there is a difference in tax rates. Now that GST will come, this difference between states will vanish. It would help to remove the tax difference as a bias, thereby helping businesses (Rupa, 2017).

Disadvantages of GST

- There will be dual control on every business by Central and State Government. So compliance cost will go up.
- All credit will be available on from online connectivity with GST Network. Hence, small businesses may find it difficult to use the system.
- VAT and service tax on some products may become higher than the current levels.
- States may lose autonomy to change their tax rates.
- Manufacturing states would lose big revenue.
- Service sector may oppose because they have to register in every state with central and state government. So every business at all

India level will have around 60 registrations while they are having just one today. Moreover, their rates will also go up.

- Retail business may oppose because their taxes will go up and they will also have to deal with Central Government now in addition to States (Rupa, 2017).

Managerial Implementation

GST has the following implications

- GST will widen the tax base, improve tax compliance and will remove unhealthy competition among states. It will redistribute the burden of taxation equitably among manufacturing and services.
- It ensures uniformity of tax system across the states. It will integrate the tax base and allow seamless flow of Input Tax Credit resulting in reduced cost of goods and services.
- It will improve disclosure of economic transactions.
- It will mitigate cascading and double taxation thus enables better compliance. It will also lead to transparency in tax system resulting in difficulty of tax evasion.
- Ensure better compliance due to aggregate tax rate reduces.
- By reducing the tax burden, the competitiveness of Indian products in international market is expected to increase and there by development of the nation.
- Prices of goods are expected to reduce in the long run as the benefits of less tax burden would be passed on to the consumer.
- GST is structured to reduce manufacturing costs. This makes • GST also means cheaper goods; fairer prices for consumers Kanchan, Nov 2016 (Shah & Joshi, 2017).

Goods and Services Tax" Network

According Wikipedia, as per the government website on GST, "Goods and Services Tax Network"is a non-profit organisation proposed to be formed for creating a website / platform for all the concerned parties related to the GST, namely stakeholders, government and taxpayers to collaborate on a single portal. When up and running, the portal is supposed to be accessible to the central government which allows it to track down every transaction on its end while taxpayers are advertised to have the ability of connecting this to their tax returns.

GST Council

The GST council is the key decision-making body that will take all important decisions regarding the GST. Council dictates tax rate, tax exemption, the due date of forms, tax laws, and tax deadlines, keeping in mind special rates and provisions for some states. The predominant responsibility of the GST Council is to ensure to have one uniform tax rate for goods and services across the nation.

The Goods and Services Tax is governed by the GST Council. Article 279 (1) of the amended Indian Constitution states that the GST Council has to be constituted by the President within 60 days of the commencement of the Article 279A. According to the article, GST Council will be a joint forum for the Centre and the States. It consists of the following members:

- The Union Finance Minister, Arun Jaitley will be the Chairperson
- As a member, the Union Minister of State will be in charge of Revenue of Finance
- The Minister in charge of finance or taxation or any other Minister nominated by each State government, as members.

Article 279A (4) specifies that the Council will make recommendations to the Union and the States on the important issues related to GST, such as, the goods and services will be subject or exempted from the Goods and Services Tax. The GST Council meets to discuss and lay GST laws that will benefit dealers across the nation. The Council will also set up anti-profiteering screening committees that will make the National Anti-Profiteering Authority stronger under the GST law. GST Council office is set up in New Delhi (Source: https://cleartax.in/s/gst-council).

The GST Council in its 23rd meeting on November 10, 2017 recommended widespread changes in the Goods and Services Tax (GST). The council has decided to keep the highest 28 per cent tax on on luxury and sinful items as a result 177 items have been shifted to the 18 per cent bracket. GST on many items have also been reduced. The government has categorised items in five major slabs - 0 per cent, 5 per cent, 12 per cent, 18 per cent and 28 per cent.

GST Returns

GST returns must be filed by all persons who register themselves under GST. There are many different kinds of GST returns that must be filed every month, according to the CGST Act, 2017. Even an annual return has to be filed by all those who are registered under GST. Entities registered under the GST Composition Scheme will have to file their returns on a quarterly basis as well as annually. The most common returns that must be filed include GSTR 1, GSTR 2, and GSTR 3.

Normal taxpayers will have to submit these three returns on a monthly basis along with one annual return, as per the CGST law. Taxpayers who are registered as Input Service Distributors are liable to collect or deduct the tax (TCS/TDS). All registered taxable individuals are required to submit outward supply information in Form GSTR 1 by the 10th day of the following month.

All registered dealers should file their returns for the specified tax period. Even in case there are no business activities during the prescribed tax period, the registered dealers are expected to file their returns. PSUs and government entities that do not engage in GST supplies or individual who deal exclusively in nil-rated/exempted/non-GST products or services. GST returns can be filed only via the online mode. Offline preparation of returns can also be done, and individuals who choose the offline route will have to upload their returns onto the portal. Here are the forms that need to be filled in and submitted:

- GST PCT 1: Application for enrolling as a Goods and Service Tax practitioner.
- GST PCT 2: Application for Enrolment Certificate for Goods and Service Tax practitioner.
- GST PCT 3: Show cause notice for disqualification.
- GST PCT 4: Order of rejection of application for enrolment as GST practitioner / or disqualification to function as a GST practitioner.
- GST PCT 5: Authorisation / withdrawal of authorisation of a Goods and Service Tax practitioner. (Source: https://www.bankbazaar.com/tax/gst.html

GST Rates in India

Most of the commodities and services that are subject to GST have been categorised under four tax slabs, viz. 5 per cent, 12 per cent, 18 per cent, and 28 per cent. However, GST Rates is not applicable to some goods and services, such as jute, fish, eggs, fresh meat, milk, chicken, curd, fresh fruits, butter milk, vegetables, natural honey, bread, salt, besan, prasad, sindoor, printed books, bindi, judicial papers, newspapers, handloom, bangles, horn cores, bone meal, bone grist, horn meal, hoof meal, palmyra jaggery, cereal grains hulled, colouring and drawing books, etc. Here is a list of goods and services under the different tax slabs:

Commodities subject to 5 per cent GST

- Agarbatti
- Apparels up to Rs 1,000
- Braille paper
- Braille typewriters
- Braille watches
- Cashew nuts
- Coir mats
- Domestic LPG
- Edible oils
- Fertilizers
- First day covers
- Fish fillet
- Floor covering
- Footwear up to Rs 500
- Frozen vegetables
- Hearing aids
- Insulin
- Matting
- Medicines
- Milk food for babies
- Packaged food items
- Packed paneer
- Pizza bread
- Postage stamps
- Revenue stamps
- Roasted coffee beans
- Rusk
- Sabudana
- Skimmed milk
- Spices
- Stamp-post marks
- Stent

- Sugar
- Tea

Services Subject to 5 per cent GST

- Transport services such as airways and railways
- Air travel in economy class
- Sale of advertisement space for print media
- Supply of tour operators' services
- Road transport by radio taxis and motor cabs
- Small restaurants earning turnover up to Rs 50 lakhs

Commodities Subject to 12 per cent GST

- Almonds
- Animal fat sausage
- Apparel above Rs 1000
- Ayurveda medicines
- Bhujia
- Butter
- Cake servers
- Carom board
- Chess board
- Chutney
- Diagnostic kits and reagents
- Exercise books
- Fish knives
- Forks
- Frozen meat products
- Fruit juice
- Fruits
- Ghee
- Glasses for corrective spectacles and flint buttons
- Jelly
- Jam
- Ladles
- Ludo
- Mobile

- Murabba
- Namkeen
- Non-AC restaurants
- Notebooks
- Nuts
- Packaged dry fruits
- Packed coconut water
- Pickle
- Playing cards
- Preparations of vegetables
- Sewing machine
- Skimmers
- Spoons
- State-run lotteries
- Tongs
- Tooth powder
- Umbrella
- Work contracts

Services Subject to 12 per cent GST

- Air tickets by business class
- Guest houses, inns, and hotels with room tariff ranging between Rs 1000 and Rs 2500 per night.

Commodities Subject to 18 per cent GST

- Aluminium foil Furniture
- Bamboo
- Bidi Patta
- Biscuits
- Branded garments
- Cakes
- Camera
- CCTV
- Circuits
- Computers

- Corn flakes
- Curry paste
- Electrical transformer
- Envelopes
- Flavoured refined sugar
- Footwear priced above Rs 500
- Hair oil
- Headgear
- Ice cream
- Instant food mixes
- Kajal pencil sticks
- Mayonnaise
- Mineral water
- Mixed condiments
- Mixed seasonings
- Monitors
- Optical Fiber
- Padding pools
- Swimming pools
- Pasta
- Pastries
- Preserved vegetables
- printed
- Printers
- Salad dressings
- Soap
- Soups
- Speakers
- Steel products
- Tampons
- Tissues
- Toiletries
- Toothpaste
- Weighing machinery (non-electrical or electronic)

Services Subject to 18 per cent GST

- AC hotels serving alcohol to customers
- Guest houses, inns and hotels with room tariff ranging from Rs 2500 and Rs 5000 per night
- IT services
- Telecom services

Commodities Subject to 28 per cent GST

- Aerated water
- After shave
- Aircraft for personal use
- Automobiles Motorcycles
- Bidis
- Ceramic tiles
- Chewing gum Molasses
- Chocolates devoid of cocoa
- Deodorants
- Dishwasher
- Dye
- Hair clippers
- Hair shampoo Sunscreen
- Paint
- Pan masala
- Shavers
- Shaving creams
- Vacuum cleaner
- Vending machines
- Waffles and wafers coated with chocolate
- Wallpaper
- Washing machine
- Water heater
- Weighing machine ATM

Services Subject to 28 per cent GST

- Gambling and race club betting

- Cinema and entertainment
- 5-star hotels
- Guest houses, inns and hotels with room tariff of Rs 5000 and upwards

(**Source:** https://www.bankbazaar.com/tax/gst.html)

Opinion of GST

When the Narendra Modi government rolled out India's goods and services tax July, 2017, the aim was to replace multiple state and federal taxes with one, simple indirect tax system. According to a recent survey of wholesalers, and retailer's businesses by Wydr, India's largest mobile-based wholesale marketplace, 57 per cent of the respondents said they don't fully understand how the GST works—and nearly one in five said they still do not understand the tax policy at all. About 1.9 million GST registrants in the country are small businesses that contribute little to the government's cash-box but still face calls for compliance.

Wydr's survey findings are a testament to tough times: Over half the respondents said they experienced a decline in sales and revenues after the introduction of the GST. More than two-thirds recorded a decline in profit. Over a quarter said profits dropped by 30 per cent or above. Though the GST was meant to put an end to a cascading and complex tax structure, nearly a third of the respondents don't believe it simplified anything. Businesses, too, are hopeful, with 45 per cent saying the GST will be good in the long run. Over half also said that they believe the resultant uniformity will make one aspect of business easier—expanding to other states.

Taxpayers are anxious about the apparent increase in tax rates after GST rollout. Consumers are apprehensive this would result in increase in prices, despite the government insisting quite the opposite. The consumers do not have to fear as it is the hidden taxes unified under the new tax regime and mentioned in the invoice handed to the buyer.

Effects of GST

According Mehra, (2017), "GST or Goods and Services Tax is going to launch in India by July and will replace the currently active indirect taxes. Implanting GST is going to be a revolutionary step after economic liberation of India. GST is a boost competitiveness and performance in India's manufacturing sector. Declining exports and high infrastructure spending are just some of the concerns of this sector. Multiple indirect taxes had also increased the administrative costs for manufacturers and distributors and with GST in place, the compliance burden has eased and this sector will grow more strongly.

GST is stated to be one of the biggest tax reforms in India, which would not only impact the businesses but also the common man. The primary impact to be felt by the consumers would change in prices of goods and services on account of GST rates. In terms of impact in prices, while services would mostly be more expensive in the initial phases, impact on prices of goods could be a mixed bag. In the long run, once the benefits of GST are expected to kick in in terms of higher input credits and reduction in cascading effect, it is anticipated that the inflationary effect will come down and prices, in general, would come down and stabilize. In services, the tax rate has increased from 15 per cent to 18 per cent.

GST is expected to bring greater transparency, improve compliance levels and create a common playing field for businesses by amalgamating a host of central and local taxes. It would change the current tax regime of production-based taxation to a consumption-based system (The Economic Times, Aug.11, 2017).The Goods and Services Tax is another such undertaking that is expected to provide the much needed stimulant for economic growth in India by transforming the existing base of indirect taxation towards the free flow of goods and services. GST is also expected to eliminate the cascading effect of taxes. India is projected to play an important role in the world economy in the years to come. The expectation of GST being introduced is high not only within the country, but also within neighbouring countries and developed economies of the world.

Effects of GST on various sectors are

- **Real estate:**GST replace all the multiple taxes that currently a buyer and a builder pays for a property. The builder pays off various taxes such as CST, entry tax, custom duty and other taxes during property procurement. The property buyers than pay service tax, VAT and other taxes on purchasing the property. All the multiple taxation system will be replaced with GST and the tax credit flow will become smooth than now.
- **Textile sector:**Currently tax imposed on textile industry vary from four per cent to 12 per cent depending on the categories. Currently taxation system in textile industry is quite unorganised as many of the supplier and manufacturer are not liable to pay tax due to their small sizes. Even, different fabric has different tax

rate levied on them. However, with GST implementation, all these differences will be collaborated under one uniform taxation system. These will result into a boom in textile exports from India."

- **Vehicle industry:** Under current taxation system, vehicle industry has different rates of taxes levied on different category which varies from 27 per cent to 45 per cent. Also excise duty is different for different types of vehicle. Under GST system, a uniform tax rate will apply on all types of car and it is expected to have a boom in automobile sale after GST implementation. However, luxury cars may get taxed at a higher rate but it is expected that small cars will be keep in the standard goods category and will be taxed at a lower rate.
- **Non-resident Indians:** With the implementation of GST impacting positively on sectors such as logistics, warehousing, automobiles, film production, DTH (direct-to-home TV), multiplexes, etc., it will make India an attractive destination for investment into these sectors by NRIs. NRIs can avoid multiple taxations amounting to indirect taxes from both state and central systems. NRIs involved in export businesses have an advantage in that, GST is not applicable to goods and services exported from India. A big incentive to the NRI community is bringing the myriad tax departments under one umbrella, thereby improving compliance and simplifying an NRI's investment process (Visal, 2017).
- **Agriculture:** The agricultural sector is the largest contributing sector the overall Indian GDP. It covers around 16 per cent of Indian GDP. One of the major issues faced by the agricultural sector is the transportation of agri-products across state lines all over India. GST will resolve the issue of transportation.
- **Telecommunications:** In the telecom sector, prices will come down after GST. Manufacturers will save on costs through efficient management of inventory and by consolidating their warehouses. Handset manufacturers will find it easier to sell their equipment as GST has negated the need to set up state-specific entities, and transfer stocks. The will also save up on logistics costs.
- **Pharma:** On the whole, GST is benefiting the pharma and healthcare industries. It will create a level playing field for generic drug makers, boost medical tourism and simplify the tax structure. If there is any concern whatsoever, then it relates to the

pricing structure (as per latest news). The pharma sector is hoping for a tax respite as it will make affordable healthcare easier to access by all.

- **E-commerce:** The e-commerce sector in India has been growing by leaps and bounds. In many ways, GST help the e-com sector's continued growth but the long-term effects will be particularly interesting because the GST law specifically proposes a Tax Collection at Source (TCS) mechanism, which e-com companies are not too happy with. The current rate of TCS is at one per cent. E-commerce websites such as Flipkart and Amazon.in will have to collect TCS (tax collected at source) at a fixed one per cent rate, and pay this collection to the sellers listed on their websites. This is likely to impact prices and make online shopping more expensive (Kashyap, 2017).

What will get costlier in the GST regime?

With GST in place the following will get costlier:

- Accommodation in hotels would attract 28 per cent GST where the room tariff is more than Rs 7,500 per unit per day
- Air-conditioned restaurants serving/not serving liquor would attract GST at the rate of 18 per cent.
- Renting of a motor car would attract GST at the rate of 18 per cent.
- Under-construction immovable property being flats, commercial buildings, etc., would attract GST at the rate of 18 per cent after allowing deduction of land value to the extent of one-third of the total amount of immovable property (Vasal, 2017).

PART - II
DEMONITIZATION

Chapter - 4

Demonetization: An Overview

A country's real economic growth rate, real GDP, formal financial system without corruption, black money and counterfeit currency are the indications for its strong formal economy. It helps for development of the economy. The meaning of demonetization is to declare a currency status from legal tender to invalid. Demonetization is done when a country wants to change its currency. New currencies are issued by calling back the old currencies. The aim of demonetization is to eliminate black money, control tax evasion, and control terrorist financing activity while promoting the country to become a cashless economy (Dcosta et. al., 2017).

The government has initiated a war against corruption, black money and eliminating fake currency through the demonetization activity. Due to the demonetization activity there are several implications that have to be faced by the average middle class people, farmers, all types of retailer and wholesaler, service renders and the economy as a whole. The demonetization had a great significant and immediate impact on the state of the Indian economy. Demonetization is the process where government declares the currently running currency notes illegal to be tender after the declaration is made. There are both pros and cons of demonetization in the Indian economy (Veerakumar, 2017).

Demonetization can be doing in such a way that it helps for averting the economic crisis. An economic crisis affects the factors determining mental health. Protective factors are weakened and risk factors strengthened. Employment benefits mental health (9). Job security, sense of control of work and social support at work are factors promoting the mental health of employee. The greater vulnerability of the disadvantaged people in each community to mental health problems may be explained by such factors as the experience of insecurity and hopelessness, poor education, unemployment, indebtedness, social isolation and poor housing.

Table 4.1. Determinants of Population Mental Health

Protective factors	*Risk factors*
Social capital and welfare protection. Healthy prenatal and childhood environment. Healthy workplace and living. Healthy lifestyles	Poverty, poor education, deprivation, high debt. Poor prenatal nutrition, abuse, harsh upbringing, poor relationship to parents, intergenerational transmission of mental health problems. Unemployment, job insecurity, job stress. Alcohol and/or drug use.

Source: Impact of economic crises on mental health; World Health Organization Report, p. 4.

The health sector cannot achieve good mental health alone. The determinants of mental health are often outside the remit of the health system, and all government sectors have to be involved in promoting mental health. Women and children feel the effects of an economic crisis. Families with low income are especially hurt by cuts in health and education budgets. Family strain may lead to increases in family violence and child neglect.

What is Demonetization?

Demonetization is the act of stripping a currency unit of its status as legal tender. Demonetization is necessary whenever there is a change of national currency. The old unit of currency must be retired and replaced with a new currency unit. Demonetization is the withdrawal of a particular form of currency from circulation. This is usually done whenever there is a change of national currency, replacing the old unit with a new one.

Demonetization is the act of stripping a currency unit of its status as legal tender. It occurs whenever there is a change of national currency. The current forms of money are pulled from circulation and are often to be replaced with new notes or coins. Sometimes a country completely replaces the old currency with new currency (Kokila & Usha devi, 2017).

The dictionary meaning of Demonetize is "To deprive (a metal) of its capacity as a monetary standard" or "To withdraw from use as currency" So, demonetization is the act of stripping a currency unit of its status as legal tender. It is the act or process of removing the legal status of currency unit. A currency on which Governor of RBI on behalf of Central Government guarantees by making statement "I promises to pay the bearer, the sum of money…" which empowers it a legal status. From the date of demonetization, all old currencies which are demonetized will cease to be a legal tender. Such currency cannot be used as money to do any transaction henceforth, but to replace with a new currency (Muthulakshmi & Kalaimani, 2017). The current form or forms of money is pulled from circulation and retired, often to be replaced with new notes or coins. Sometimes, a country completely replaces the old currency with new currency.

As example of demonetization we can remember Coinage Act of 1873 demonetized silver as the legal tender of the United States, in favor of fully adopting the gold standard. Several coins, including two-cent piece, three-cent piece, and half dime were discontinued. The withdrawal of silver from the economy resulted in a contraction of the money supply, which subsequently led to a five-year economic depression throughout the country. In 2016, the Indian government decided to demonetize the 500- and 1000-rupee notes, the two biggest denominations in its currency system; these notes accounted for 86 per cent of the country's circulating cash. With little warning, India's Prime Minister Narendra Modi announced to the citizenry on Nov. 8 that those notes were worthless, effective immediately – and they had until the end of the year to deposit or exchange them for newly introduced 2000 rupee and 500 rupee bills (Source: Investopedia).

Aim of Demonetization

The main aim of demonetization is to curb the black money, corruption, terrorism and fake currencies in India. In India, mostly people use cash transactions and it is misused by some bad elements of the society. The introduction of demonetization addresses black money issues and also helps to increase the digital economy in India. It has similar impacts on the terror activities financing in India and also corruption that exists in India (Dcosta et. al., 2017). Deodhar (2016) highlighted that the demonetization of Rs 500 and Rs 1000 by the government was targeted towards tackling black money, corruption and terrorism.

With a view to curb financing of terrorism through the proceeds of Fake Indian Currency Notes (FICN) and use of such funds for subversive activities such as espionage, smuggling of arms, drugs and other contrabands into India, it was decided to cancel the legal tender character of the High Denomination bank notes. The reason for 2016 demonetization in India was, (a) to eliminate counterfeit currency, (b) to shrink the size of the parallel economy and black money in India, (c) to reduce corruption and (d) To curtail terror financing (Preethi & Sangeetha, 2017).

In his different speech on demonetization Indian Prime Minister Narendra Modi clearly, points out that this bold step has been taken to get a control over corruption in the country. Secondly, it is done to curb black money, thirdly it is also a step to control escalating price rise, fourth to stop fund flow to illegal activity. On the other hand, demonetization in India is also a very well planned step of govt of India to earn proper tax from the citizen.

The main objective of demonetization is to motivate cash less economy and fight against black money. It has following objectives:

- It's a blast on black money by transmit cash into bank accounts. It purposes to change the tradition of off-thebook transactions in the country. It is requiring, encouraging to taxations and the country's income.
- It aims to drag the carpet from under the pes of those circulating fake notes, which disrupt the economy. Use such notes stimulate terrorism and drug trafficking.
- It promotes to the move near a cashless society and digital economy, which is more efficient. It reduces transaction costs in a range of areas from payments to loans. This can contribute toward innovation and growth.
- Removal of big currency is the first step in preventing illegal financial activities.
- This demonetization promotes the plastic money or online payment systems. In which alteration is unavoidable so, all the financial transactions acceptable only the use of cards, electronic and paper money.
- Its purpose to stop scamper the funding which is used in illegitimate actions (Chaudhary et. al., 2017).

Demonetization in Countries

- **Russia:** On its last legs, the country under Mikhail Gorbachev in January 1991 withdrew large-ruble bills from circulation in a move to take on the black economy. The reform failed to halt inflation, and instead served mainly to accelerate a slide in public confidence in the government. As political infighting combined with economic collapse, Gorbachev faced a coup attempt that August which destroyed his authority and led to the Soviet break-up the following year. Learning lessons, Russia's 1998 redenomination of the rubble, when it removed three zeroes, went altogether more smoothly.

- **North Korea:** In 2010, the regime of then-dictator Kim Jong-Il mounted a reform that knocked off two zeros from the face value of the old currency in an effort to tighten control of the economy and close black markets. Combined with a poor harvest, the measure left the country with severe food shortages, according to reports at the time. Surging rice prices stoked unrest that prompted an unusual apology from Kim, and — reports suggested — the execution of the ruling party's head of finance. North Korea has taken confiscatory steps to curb unofficial economic activity and suppress inflation, issuing a revalued currency and sharply limiting the amount of old money people can exchange for new bills. The measures appeared to be a crude form of shock therapy intended to severely punish people involved in black market trading, which had begun to take root in North Korea in recent years as the country's central planning system broke down (CHOE SANG-HUN, 2009).
- **Zaire:** Dictator Mobutu Sese Seko faced increasing economic disruptions in the early 1990s, when his administration mounted successive banknote reforms. A plan to withdraw obsolescent currency from the system in 1993 saw a surge in inflation and a collapse in the exchange rate against the dollar. After a civil war, Mobutu was ousted in 1997.
- **Myanmar:** In 1987, the country's military junta invalidated as much as 80 per cent of the value of money in circulation, according to reports at the time — as in other such initiatives, it was directed at curbing the black market. One result was the first student demonstrations in years. Deepening economic unease helped trigger mass protests across the nation the following year that led to a government crackdown that killed thousands of people (Muthulakshmi & Kalaimani, 2017).
- **Pakistan:** Pakistan's Senate Monday passed a resolution seeking withdrawal of high denomination Rs 5,000 currency notes "in a phased manner" to curb the flow of black money, weeks after India demonetised its high value currencies. The resolution said that the withdrawal of Rs 5,000 notes will encourage the use of bank accounts and reduce the size of the undocumented economy, Dawn reported. It said the withdrawal of the currency notes

should take place within three to five years in order to purge markets of the notes. Law Minister Zahid Hamid, however, said that the withdrawal of the notes will create crises in the market and the people will resort to foreign currencies in absence of Rs 5,000 notes. He said that currently 3.4 trillion notes are in circulation in country of which 1.02 trillion notes are of Rs 5,000 denominations.

Table 4.2: Facts about Demonetization in Different nations across the Globe

Country	*Year*	*Step Taken*	*Status*
United States of America	1969	Due to black money existence in nation, the country was losing its sheen built on Silicon Valley and the so-called even today existent American Dream. In 1969, US President Richard Nixon announced all bills above $100 null and void.	Success. Even today $100 bill is the maximum available for circulation.
Nigeria	1984	The government run by Muhammadu Buhari has announced demonetization of all existing currencies to improve the high-inflation-debt economy,	Failed. He was thrown out of power in 1985-86.
Zaire	1990	The Dictator Mobutu ran the demonetization drive which led to economic instability in the country which won freedom in 1970 making it more vulnerable to foreign funding at that time. The country recovered in 2000.	Failed.
Soviet Union	January 1991	Mikhail Gorbachev, withdrew 50 and 100 ruble notes, in order to eliminate black money and increase the currency value. The notes accounted for a third of the total money in circulation.	Gorbachev faced a coup within eight months in August as the move was not a success. The 1991 attempt led to a successful re-denomination of the rubble in 1998 where three zeros were removed. This was followed by another currency switch in 2010 when two more zeros were removed from the old currency. The 2010 attempt was not as successful as the timing coincided with a poor harvest.
Australia	1996	The government to the curb black money crisis and improve security features on the notes, they withdrew all paper-based notes and replaced them with long life polymer-based notes of the same denomination.	Success. This improved the life of the bills and helped in making Australia a business friendly country, despite the initial costs incurred to manufacture polymer based notes.

(*Contd...*)

Zimbabwe	2010	Due to chronic inflation in Zimbabwe, the government started printing notes with a face value of 1 hundred trillion Zimbabwean Dollars' worth just 40 cents.	Failed. The country replaced their currency with US Dollars later.
North Korea	2010	The then dictator of North Korea Kim Jong-IL has decided to remove two zeroes from the currency denominations to curb black money menace and tightly control the economy	Miserably Failed. Due to bad harvest and high inflation, this move was highly criticized by the International Media, making the dictator to apologize in the public.
Pakistan	June, 2015	The Government of Pakistan has announced the demonetization of Rs.5 and Rs.500 in June 2015 with immediate effect and phase out of all other denominations. The people of Pakistan had oneand-half year time to exchange these notes, after which (December 1, 2016) the notes will be declared null and void.	Messed Up. One and Half Years for demonetization. To exchange notes. Can't curb black money neither counterfeit notes.
Venezuela	Dec 11,2016	The president of the country Nicolas Maduro signed an emergency decree ordering the country's largest banknote, 100 Bolivar bill, to be illegal tender within 72 hours. This was a step to curb the hoarding of cash by international "mafia".	Forced to take it back after chaos & death of a person.

Source: Shirley, A. (2017). Impact of Demonetization in India, Special Issue Published in International Journal of Trend in Research and Development, pp. 22-23.

From the table above we find the demonetization done by developed nations have been successful and African nations have suffered a lot because these countries are still a victim of neo-colonialism.

Merits of Demonetization

Various merits of demonization with respect to Indian Government demonetization in 2016 are:

- **Rise of The Cashless Economy:** Spread of the digital payment culture will start the 'formalization' process in the economy. It will reduce the use of physical cash as well. Once bulk of the economic transactions is digitalized it will result in revealing the expenditure made by individuals to the tax authorizes especially big transactions. Pushing India towards becoming a cashless economy was another reason that demonetization was publicized for. People turned towards digital transactions for everything from buying groceries from a road side vendor to paying utility bills during the time of demonetization. However, as the flow of cash into the economy began to increase, the use of these apps and digital wallets saw a slide once again (Krishnan, 2017).

- **Growth of The Formal Economy:** If additional measures like cleaning the real estate sector and brining all traders under the digital payment system, the unorganized sector transaction will be made accountable. Even if it is a slow process, bringing the informal sector into the formal economy will reduce black money.
- **Social Shake Up:** Black money can be eliminated only if we eliminate the deep rooted social mentality that dealing with black money is economically rewarding and legally feasible. Demonetization may bring a social shake up in the country by destroying this mentality. It will spread an attitude against black money. People will be averse to deal with black money if they know that they are easily traceable and harder legal steps are initiated against them. Such an awareness and conscience can reduce the area available for the activation of black money.
- **Controlling Parallel Economy:** Demonetization is not an isolate arm or not only one against black money. It may be complemented by several other steps. One such supportive step is making PAN compulsory for high value transactions up to Rs 10000. Similarly, PAN documentation should be made compulsory against all investment in physical assets like gold, land etc., if these happens, parallel economic activities can be reduced substantially. In the country about Rupees Five Lakh Crore black money is existing in the economy. The Narendra Modi government has introduced demonetization to curb the black money. The cash circulation in the country is directly proportional to the corruption rate. So in order to lower the corruption rate the cash circulation in the country has been reduced. The demonetization also helps in eradicating fake currencies and suspicious funds which are mainly used to find terrorism in the country (Kiruthiga & Magesh, 2016).
- **Large Number of New Tax Payers:** It will increase number of tax payers.This is because demonetized money will reveal their income size and tax officials may check them in future, compelling to pay tax (Sangeetha, 2017).
- **Hawala transactions:**Demonetisation has crippled the hawala rackets. Hawala is a method of transferring money without any actual money movement. Hawala route is used as a means to facilitate money laundering and terror financing. Hawala rackets run again on black money. With black money suddenly being wiped out of the market, thanks to demonetisation, hawala

operations have come to a grinding halt. According to an India Today report, one of the hawala operators in Mumbai has destroyed currency notes worth about Rs 500 crores.

- **Real estate cleansing:** It is said that real estate is an industry built on black money. The extent of black money floating around in the sector is huge. According to an estimate at least 40 per cent of real estate transactions in Delhi-NCR are in black. Modi's demonetisation move will curtail the flow of black money into the real estate sector. This will help in making the much needed correction in the sector. The impact: An unexpected dip in land and property price.
- **Economy:** Demonetisation will have a huge resultant effect on the Indian economy. The clean-up of illegal cash will help turn around the economy. First, it will bring more borrowings to the exchequer, improve inflation outlook and increase India's gross domestic product. Second, it will revive investment opportunities and give a fillip to infrastructure and the manufacturing sector. Third, it will help reduce interest rates and lower income tax rate.
- **Terror financing:** Terror financing is sourced through counterfeit currency and hawala transactions. This is how terror financing works. Fake currency circulation is routed through a multi-layered network of hawala operators which are closely linked to satta (gambling) and smuggling of drugs, opium and arms. Indirectly, they all end up financing terrorism. In addition, the terrorists collect huge donations and then route the money through hawala transactions. With the circulation of counterfeit Indian currency completely stalled and hawala transactions stopped, all windows for terror financing are closed.
- **Maoism:** Maoist sympathisers call Modi's demonetisation move an "undeclared financial emergency". There are reasons to it. Demonetisation has hit the Maoists and their movement hard. Black money is the oxygen for Maoists. According to an estimate, Maoists manage to raise Rs 300 to Rs 400 crore annually through donations, levy and extortions. The illicit money is used to purchase arms and ammunition, food and medicine and daily essentials, apart from distributing it among the ranks and the cadre.
- **Kashmir Unrest:** The four-month-long unrest in Kashmir valley is on a backburner, thanks to demonetisation. No stone pelting on

security forces has been reported in Kashmir ever since the demonetisation announcement was made. An intelligence estimate suggests that Pakistan sends Rs 1,000 crore annually to the separatists for fuelling unrest in Kashmir. The money is transferred through hawala route. With Hawala transactions completely choked up, the separatists are now clueless. It won't be wrong to say that "stone pelter" Modi completely shattered the Kashmir unrest with his stone called demonetisation (Muthulakshmi, 2017).

- **Non-Performing Assets:** After demonetisation the possibility of diversion of funds has almost become nil. The reason being is this demonetisation not only brought the rule for exchange of 500 and 1000 rupees note but also brought the technology for tracking of new notes through satellite. Even government also makes mandatory to transfer money through banks only to make valid contracts. This is the prime reason the borrowers cannot use or invest the funds taken for a particular purpose on anywhere else. This demonetisation compelled the people to deposit their cash into bank. Now the banks are flushed with huge amount of funds which could also bring opportunities to the banks to provide sufficient amount of funds to more authentic clients who were deprived earlier. Such step lead to the less possibilities of occurring NPAs in future. Though it's a good sign for the banks that people have made huge amount of deposits due to this demonetisation which would not only help the banks in getting sufficient amount of funds but on the other hand it may also bring over capitalisation of banks (Meher, 2017).
- **Tax Payments:** Pushing Indians to deposit and account the cash lying in their house also meant a rise in the tax payments for the country. According to government reports the income tax payers saw a record increase in the post demonetization era. 9.1 million New taxpayers were added to the slab which was an 80 per cent rise over the typical yearly rise. This increase in the number of taxpaying citizens in the country has been credited to demonetization. This increase was also resonated in IT returns filing and advance tax payment (Krishnan, 2017).

Demerits of Demonetization

- **Liquidity Crunch (short term effect):** Liquidity shock means people are not able to get sufficient volume of popular denomination especially Rs 500. This currency unit is the favourable denomination in daily life. It constituted to nearly 49 per cent of the previous currency supply in terms of value. Higher the time required to resupply Rs 500 notes, higher will be the duration of the liquidity crunch. Current reports indicate that all security printing press can print only 2000 million units of Rs 500 notes by the end of this year. Nearly 16000 mn Rs 500 notes were in circulation as on end March 2016. Some portion of this were filled by the new Rs 2000 notes.

- **Welfare Loss for the Currency using Population:** Most active segments of the population who constitute the 'base of the pyramid' uses currency to meet their transactions. The daily wage earners, other labourers, small traders etc. who reside out of the formal economy uses cash frequently. These sections will lose income in the absence of liquid cash. Cash stringency will compel firms to reduce labour cost and thus reduces income to the poor working class (Kasthuri, 2017).
- **Hurdles due to Demonetization:**The March 2016 report of the Reserve Bank of India revealed that the currency circulation in the country is Rs 16,415 billion. Out of which Rs 500 notes accounted to 47.30 per cent in value and the Rs 1000 notes account to 38.60 per cent. They constitute 85.90 per cent of the circulated money value. So, it's a very huge amount to be frozen at a single stretch. Although the government has given reason for demonetization as curbing black money, the actual generation and storage of black money is through foreign currency. Actually the current demonetization affects small traders, vendors, daily wage labourers and fishermen are some who are mostly affected. It has created a harassing situation to the ordinary people who want to change their currency. The issue of Rs 2000 denomination notes is of no use for lower and middle class people. If they are purchasing for Rs 600, they should get a change of Rs 1400. It is really hard to get change for Rs 2000 note (Kiruthiga & Magesh, 2016).
- **Social Impacts:** The information on demonetization was released suddenly and the worst affected was the common man. The social impact was drastic with marriages facing severe issues with cash transactions in marriages coming to a standstill. People conducting marriages must produce the marriage invitation to withdraw 2,50,000 and above. This has caused great hassles among the public. The impact on the health care sector was huge with most of the hospitals refused to accept the old currency. The issue was

faced by the Union Minister Mr. Sidharamaiah in Bengaluru when the hospital administration refused to accept the old currency to retrieve his brother's dead body. The common man faced severe issues transacting in the hospitals with old currencies and several cases of death have been registered for not attending the patients due to demonetization (Dash, 2017).

- **Impact on Banks:** The All India Bank Officers Association had given a call for demonstration against the problems that various banks and their employees were facing due to demonetization. Bank employees are feeling increasingly targeted in the face of public anger. The constant notifications and the lack of cash provided have led banking establishments facing the wrath of clients. Banks staff members serve the people and are working overtime to keep their commitments, but are helpless when they do not get enough cash to meet the minimum requirement of the customers. Public sector bank officers are being subjected to the anger, anguish and wrath of customers or general public due to short supply of currency notes to the banks. There is acute shortage of Rs 100 currency notes and hence even the recalibrated ATMs are not able to dispense cash to the customers (Dash & Bagha, 2017).
- **Small farmers:** The Governments move to introduce the 2000/- in new currency to ease the money shortfall has not helped because small buyer have been left with a big currency that nobody wanted to exchange. Those who had cash are using it prudently and only if is absolutely necessary because they did not want to go through the ordeal of standing in long queues at banks for cash withdrawals. This has led to a lot of hardship to small traders who do not have large holding capacities and need to sell per day to meet their family needs. Cultivation also badly affected because due to cancellation of old currency and shortage of money they are unable to purchase fertilizer, seed, pesticides for cultivation (Bhattacharyya & Mehta, 2016).
- **Gross Domestic Product:** The ban on old notes is being cited as one of the key contributors to the economic slowdown. With the gross domestic product for the April-June quarter slipping to 5.7 per cent, the reality of the economic slowdown could not be ignored. The World Bank has reduced the India GDP growth forecast to seven per cent for 2017-18 owing to demonetization and GST (Goods and Service tax). The slowdown is being cited as

a delayed consequence of demonetization by the World Bank and while there are various other reasons at play, the steep decline has been credited to be an effect of demonetization (Krishnan, 2017).

- **Loss of Life:** A lot of people struggled, died as direct and indirect effects of demonetization. Hospitals, clinics, sellers were not accepting the old money in the transition period. Some of them exhausted in the long queue under the hot sun, some injured in the agitations. This is one the biggest problem in demonetization implementation (Sueniel, 2017).
- **Political Game:** Every political party in opposition stood against the present government, they agitated showing that they are on people's side. It shows that no matter what been done for good of the nation, political parties in opposition will oppose it by taking the name of common on but working for own political agenda in mind. This shows for politicians the political game is more important than the nation (Sueniel, 2017).

Chapter - 5

Demonetization in India

India's demonetisation is unprecedented in international economic history, in that it combined secrecy and suddenness amidst normal economic and political conditions. India's action is not unprecedented in its own economic history: there were two previous instances of demonetisation, in 1946 and 1978. On November 8, 2016, the government announced a historic measure, with profound implications for the economy. The two largest denomination notes, Rs 500 and Rs 1000, were demonetized with immediate effect, ceasing to be legal tender except for a few specified purposes. The aim of the action was fourfold: to curb corruption; counterfeiting; the use of high denomination notes for terrorist activities; and especially the accumulation of black money, generated by income that has not been declared to the tax authorities. Demonetization can be said as a Surgical Strike on Black Money, Terrorism, Fake Currency, Unorganized trading, Real Estate, Share market etc. on the other hand if we talk about the Indian industry on a broader way it can be categories in three parts Manufacturing sector, Service sector and Agriculture sector (Bansal, 2017).

The public debate on demonetisation has raised three sets of questions. First, broader aspects of management, as reflected in the design and implementation of the initiative. Second, its economic impact in the short and medium run. And, third, its implications for the broader vision underlying the future conduct of economic policy (Source: Economic Survey 2016-17, Govt. of India).

Demonetization on January 1946

Two ordinances were issued by the government on January 12, 1946. The first one asked banks to share (provide) information about the currency holding in terms of notes with big denominations i.e. Rupees 500, 1000 and 10000. The second ordinance meant for public stated that notes with denomination of Rupees 500 and above were going to be demonetized and exchange with Rupees 100 denomination note within a time limit up to January 23, 1946 and later extended while conditioned that individuals would have to make clarify why they couldn't exchange the in previous limited time frame. The outcome was almost a big failure since out of total notes issued having value Rs 143.97 crore, the notes exchanged having value Rs 134.9 crore (source: www.investopedia.com).

Demonetization on January 1978

The second major demonetization move in India got momentum on January 14, 1978 announced at 9 a.m. through All India Radio. The announcement stated that within a limited time frame of three days, people could exchange their high denomination notes i.e. Rs 500, 1000 and 10000. This time, such demonetization was a futile exercise with no destroyed any money stock at all The sole aim of the ban was to curb black money generation in the country. However, the public nature of the recommendation sparked black money hoarders to act fast and rid themselves of high denominations before the government was able to clamp down on them. (source: mostlyeconomics.wordpress.com).

Demonetization on 8th November, 2016

The Government of India, on 8th November, 2016 announced demonetization of all Rs 500 and Rs 1,000 banknotes which stripped those currencies of their legal tender status. However, the lower denomination currencies Rs 10, Rs 20, Rs 50, Rs 100 and coins remained valid. This move was attempted by the government to tackle three problems in the economy viz., a parallel economy, counterfeit currency and terror financing. The Indian government's stated objective behind the 2016 demonetization policy are as follows; first, to make India corruption free, second, to curb black money, third, to control inflation, fourth, to stop terror financing, fifth, to make the people pay income tax and finally, to make a cashless society and create Digital India. The demonetization policy is seen as a financial reform in the country but this decision is fraught with its own merits and demerits (Preethi & Sangeetha, 2017).

On 8 November, 2016, Prime Minister of India Narendra Modi declared the demonetisation in an unscheduled live broadcast address to the country at 20:15 IST. Which made periled in various levels of the general public and the economy foreseeing the effect of such approach on various part of a person and additionally corporate and sectorial ions (Dash & Bagha, 2017). Indian government's goal was to remove all counterfeit (fake) currency from the market which is used in tax evasion, corruption and even in funding terrorist activities. These two currency notes are the most used currency in the Indian market, it had 86 per cent share in the market. This was a very big and risky decision and as some aptly said it is a "Masterstroke".

As per RBI, 87 per cent transactions in India are cash transactions and this loophole is used by corrupted people to build a parallel economy with unaccounted money. This parallel economy helps in terror financing which in turn hampers the growth and development of country. Currently high-value notes account for total value of 86 per cent of the notes circulation in India. It is expected that this step will help in reducing the fiscal deficit of India and promote the cashless economy in India which can be easily monitored. Demonetization creates panic among the common man, particularly among retailers and shopkeepers

By making the larger denomination notes worthless, individuals and entities with huge sums of black money gotten from parallel cash systems were forced to convert the money at a bank which is by law required to acquire tax information from the entity could not provide proof of making any tax payments on the cash, a tax penalty of 200 per cent of the tax owned was imposed (Sangeetha, 2017). All existing 500- and 1,000-rupee notes would have no value after December 30. It was expected that this measure would put an end to unaccountable stockpiles of cash. Modi acknowledged, of course, that legitimate "white" money could also be held in cash—and that people who had white-money cash holdings should not be penalized (Krishna, 2017).

The policy mechanics of demonetisation were governed by two notifications, issued by India's Ministry of Finance and the Reserve Bank of India. Both were issued shortly after Prime Minister Modi had announced the policy on national television on the evening of 8 November, 2016 and came into effect the same day at midnight. the way demonetisation was communicated is the lack of insight government bodies offered into the reasoning behind it. The RBI notification, for example, did not provide any pointers towards the rationale behind demonetisation – in spite of it being the government body that had officially recommended the policy. The little information provided by the MoF notification similarly lacked dispassionate observations and clearly defined policy goals.

One issue that dominated the Indian public discourse on demonetisation was its evolutionary nature: Between 8 November and 30 December, the last day to exchange or deposit old notes, the RBI issued 50 notifications to guide and regulate the process and to remind the actors, namely public and private sector banks, of their legal obligations. Some of these were of an advisory nature but a large proportion provided substantive changes to the workings of the policy. From the public's perspective, the most visible changes to the policy mechanics of demonetisation concerned exchanging and depositing of old notes, as well as caps on the availability of new notes. By the end of the year 2016, the RBI had issued nine notifications on the exchange and deposit process and five on cash withdrawal limits.

Apart from leading to criticism that demonetisation was, in the words of former Prime Minister Manmohan Singh, characterised by "monumental mismanagement", these frequent and often sudden policy changes had a direct impact on the population. Compounding the existing confusion about the timeframe during which old notes could be exchanged or deposited was the fact that the RBI introduced separate rules for District Central Cooperative Banks and Primary Agricultural Credit Societies, the primary financial institutions used by the rural population (Beyes & Bhattacharya, 2017).

Following the announcement by the Prime Minister the governor of the Reserve Bank of India, Urjit Patel made a press release with details on the procedure for exchanging the 500 and 1000 rupee notes that are currently in circulation. On 8 November, other than the notification that these denominations will be discontinued, there were a few other relevant announcements such as:

- Citizens will have until December 30, 2016 to tender the discontinued banknotes at any office of the RBI or any bank branch and credit the value into their respective bank accounts.
- For immediate cash needs, the discontinued banknotes of value up to 4000 per person can be exchanged for the new banknotes over the counter of bank branches from 10 November, 2016 by furnishing a valid ID proof.
- All ATMs will remain closed from midnight on 8 November, 2016. The ATMs will resume functioning from 11 November, 2016 upon their recalibration to dispense bank notes of only 50 and 100 rupee denominations.
- Banks have been advised to provide all cash withdrawal transactions at their ATMs free of cost to their customers till

30 December, 2016. Cash withdrawals from ATMs will be restricted to 2000 per day per card up to 18 November, 2016 and the limits will be raised to 4000 per day per card from 19 November, 2016.
- All banks will remain closed to the public on 9 November, 2016 (Sharif, 2016).

Important Steps taken before this announcement was made

- Jan Dhan scheme, under which 22-crore new bank accounts were opened in one-and-a-half years (May 2016), was the first truly game-changing move. Most of these accounts brought those people into the network who were outside the ambit. According to the Economic Survey for 2015-16 released in February this year, leakages in LPG subsidy transfers fell 24 per cent and the exclusion of beneficiaries had been greatly reduced, thanks to the infrastructure created by Jan Dhan accounts, Aadhaar and mobile networks, or the JAM trinity.
- The next step was to bring back black money stashed away in tax havens or foreign banks abroad and here.
- Then came the Income Declaration Scheme. By 30 September, all illegal asset holders had the chance to declare their holdings and pay 45 per cent tax and a penalty in exchange for anonymity and immunity from criminal proceedings.
- The government should come up with additional economic stimulus to offset the dampening effect: (a) Accelerated reduction in corporate income tax along with withdrawal of exemptions; (b) Ending uncertainty on GAAR and retrospective taxation or any other blockbuster measure that they might be working on, that would offset the initial adverse economic impact.
- Assess Black Money better: There's no good estimate for how much of India's black money is in forms other than currency/ physical notes such as gold, jewellery, land or any other form of wealth. Therefore, while banning Rs 500 and Rs 1,000 notes will tackle the black money that is in the form of hard cold cash, it won't affect other forms of black money.
- Prepare for the challenges of cashless economy: The UPI (unified payment interface) system is likely to be fully operationalised only by January 2017. India was recently hit by one of its biggest financial security breaches compromising hundreds of thousands of debit cards (Sharif, 2016).

Similarities in 1978 and 2016 Ban

- The note ban by Morarji Desai and Narendra Modi aimed to drive away black money out of circulation in the economy. Hence, The High Denomination Bank Notes (Demonetization) Act, 1978 was implemented.
- Narendra Modi announced the currency ban in an address that was broadcasted across all news channels. Similarly, Desai announced the ban over the radio after which the banks were closed the following day
- Both the affairs were kept confidential (Preethi & Sangeetha, 2017).

Differences in the Currency Ban

- Unlike Modi, Desai didn't have the backing of the RBI Governor. The Governor I.G. Patel believed that the ban was implemented simply to immobilize the funds of the opposition party. Patel also believed that people never store black money in the form of currency for too long.
- The 1978 currency ban affected only the privileged few, while the 2016 ban had shaken the whole country (Preethi & Sangeetha, 2017).

Decision of Demonetization is Arbitrary?

According the paper of Santoshi (2017), "The present legal tender of Rs 1000 and Rs 500 was withdrawn on 8th November, 2016 without bringing any specific legislation as was done earlier. This action of the government was challenged before the Supreme Court as well as various High Courts. The question that the legal tender character of bank notes can be withdrawn without bringing legislation is a debatable issue which can only be settled by judicial pronouncements. The scope of testing the decision to demonetize the current legal tender of bank notes is very limited.

The Supreme Court doesn't interfere in the policy making of the Government with respect to financial matters. Since it has come in public domain that the reasons for demonetization is to curb the illicit financial transactions which is affecting the economy including terrorist and naxal activities and to stop money laundering which is primarily done in high denomination notes. The growing menace of use of high denomination bank notes in betting, hawala transactions, corruption, black money, drug money will be significantly curtailed including circulation of fake currency notes The reasons given by the Government are certainly reasonable and cogent one.

If the legal tender character of Rs 500 and Rs 1000 bank notes can be withdrawn without legislation; why did the government enact law on earlier occasion? The legality will certainly be examined by the Supreme Court/ High Courts in the pending matters. Therefore, to avoid any legal lacuna, it would appropriate for the government to bring legislation and justify its actions. The Government of India has been promoting electronic transactions which are cashless to achieve the goal of transparency in trade/dealing and include majority of the population within the tax net.

Due to large scale prevalence of cash transactions, the revenue collection of the government is significantly reduced. The World Bank in July, 2010, estimated the size of the shadow economy to be about 23 per cent of the GDP in the year 2007. The shadow economy deprives the government of its legitimate revenues which the government could have used for welfare and development activities. It is expected that the decision of withdrawing legal tender character of Rs 500 and Rs 1000 bank notes will bring a significant change in all aspects in the country" (Santoshi, 2017).

Judicial Approach on Demonetization

According Santoshi (2017), a PIL challenging the Government's decision on demonetization was heard in the Chief Justice's court. The court did not grant a stay on the government's notification. Court also of the view that it will not interfere with the economic policies of the government. However, it did take notice of the inconvenience caused to the common man and asked the government to, on the next hearing (on 24th or 26th Nov), apprise it of the measures taken by it to alleviate this inconvenience.

The Centre had submitted an affidavit last week on the demonetization move in the Supreme Court, saying it is an attempt to unearth black money stashed over the last seven decades. Attorney General Mukul Rohatgi said that the Centre had filed a reply in the Supreme Court in compliance with the top court's earlier order on the issue. The Centre in its affidavit told the apex court that demonetization is a step to reduce ratio of cash transactions, adding the objective is to unearth illegal parallel economy (Santoshi, 2017),

Constitutional Validity of Demonetization in India

(a) Legal Issues

- No legislative mandate: The present demonization was carried out without any law passed by legislature. In 1978 the government demonetized the notes through ordinance.
- Misuse of RBI Act 1934: Although Section 26 of RBI act allows Central government to demonetize any series of notes, it has been contended by petitioners that government the power cannot be exercised to declare all series of notes as no legal tender.
- Violation of doctrine of legitimate expectation: Govt. is frequently changing the rules. e.g. Deadline of currency exchange was preponed to 25 November with a short duration notice despite of clearly stating the deadline of 30th December earlier (Santoshi, 2017),

(b) Constitutional Issues

- Violates Article 300A: Article 300A guarantees that no one can be deprives of his property without any authority of law. Demonetization lacks legislative mandate & restricts people in withdrawing money from banks.
- Violates Right to Equality: The demonetization notification discriminates between holder and non-holders of bank account.
- Violates Right to life: Poor people are unable to earn their livelihood due to cash crunch.
- Violates freedom of trade & occupation: Freedom to trade & occupation have suffered after demonetization. Businesses of many small vendors and sellers are affected due to currency shortage (Santoshi, 2017),

Public Reaction

According to Investopedia, soon after the announcement, people rushed to buy gold, a demand that drove prices up, in some cases even to a 60 per cent premium, prompting the tax authorities to conduct surveys, according to the Business Standard newspaper. The government emphasized the need to furnish PAN (Indian Permanent Account Number) card details on purchases for accountability purposes, and many jewelry shops that were flouting the norms came under crackdowns. Many Indians switched to alternative payment avenues – a big deal in a country of 1.2 billion with only 25.9 million credit cards and 697 million ATM cards as of July 2016. The biggest gainers were mobile wallet companies that offer ease of transactions through a large network of partners.

Prepaid cash cards were another option that customers found useful, and that meant good news for companies like ItzCash. Other alternatives include mobile payments systems linked to e-commerce businesses like Ola Money, Free Charge, Flipkart Wallet. Over 3 trillion rupees, or over $44 billion in old currency, was deposited with Indian banks in just the first week after the demonetization.

The decision was both praised and criticised by economists, other experts, politicians and common people. Right after the news spread out, a large number of people reacted on social media sites like Twitter. Several bankers like Arundhati Bhattacharya (Chairperson of State Bank of India), Chanda Kochhar (MD & CEO of ICICI Bank) and Deepak Parekh (Chairman of HDFC) appreciated the move that would help curb black money. Businessmen Anand Mahindra (Mahindra Group), Sajjan Jindal (JSW Group) and Kunal Bahal (Snapdeal and FreeCharge) welcomed the decision that would also accelerate e-commerce.

However, CM of West Bengal Mamata Banerjee called the new declaration as "drama" and tweeted "Heartless and ill- conceived blow on the common people and the middle class in the fake name of anti-corruption". Indian National Congress spokesperson Randeep Surjewala welcomed the move but showed apprehension on consequences that would follow. A Public Interest Litigation was filed in Madras High Court by M Seeni Ahamed, General Secretary of Indian National League, to scrap the decision. The High Court dismissed the PIL stating that it could not interfere in monetary policies of the government, however found the action suitable for country's security and development. Similar PILs have been filed in the Supreme Court of India (Sharif, 2016).

Experts and Economists Views

(a) Dr. Manmohan Singh

Supporters of PM Modi and his party, the Bharatiya Janata Party, hailed the edict as a good and necessary measure that "will clean up the system." Critics, though, have lambasted it as a "silly" move that caused enormous pain to Indians, particularly those in rural areas with little access to bank branch networks or ATMs. Former Prime Minister Manmohan Singh, an accomplished economist and the architect of India's economic liberalization program, even called it "organized loot" and "legalized plunder."

Talking to Bloomberg Quint, Singh also noted: "The damage it has caused has been multiple — economic, social, reputational and institutional. Slowing GDP is merely one indicator of the economic damage. Its impact on the weaker sections of our society and business is far more damaging than any economic indicator can reveal." Furthermore, Singh said, it was "an attack on the independence and credibility of the RBI as an institution," referring to India's central bank, the Reserve Bank of India.

(b) Jagdish Bhagwati

Globally acclaimed economist Jagdish Bhagwati said demonetisation will promote growth. "The Prime Minister's success in Uttar Pradesh has therefore meant that Amartya Sen and his friends who argued that demonetisation would hurt growth, have been humiliated and exposed as much as the Congress," Bhagwati told PTI in an email interview. "After BJP's victory in Uttar Pradesh, indeed Prime Minister Narendra Modi is now in an even stronger position than when he was first elected resoundingly," Bhagwati said. He also said that three things ought to be noted that made (Prime Minister Narendra Modi's) current position 'unassailable' (Source: The Indian Express, March 17, 2017).

(c) Amartya Sen

According to Indian express, Professor Amartya Sen said that millions of innocent people have deprived from their money and being suffered to get their own money back.

(d) Kaushik Basu

According to Indian express. Kaushik Basu said that government of India made policy that any person who deposits money beyond the limit of 250000, have to pay huge penalty. This policy created a new black market, in which large amount of illicit cash broken in to smaller parts and deposited by the members of team; which is a legal way of illegal activity. Mr., Basu said this move is hurting innocent people who has no illegal money but they have built up cash reserve over a long period of time.

(e) Arun Shourie

According to Indian express, Mr. Arun Shourie said in an interview with NDTV, that this note banned policy made by present Indian government is not poke on black money, because the owner of black money converted their money into tangible and intangible assets. The persons who have huge black money, they never keep money in cash, they never keep money under the mattress, or in gunny bags. They invested their black money in properties, jewelries, stock markets or in other assets.

(f) Arun Jaitley

According to Indain Express Arun Jaitley gives his opinion that the demonetization is good for economy, Indian banks were facing NPA problem since last many years, now banks will have more money to lend for many sectors of the economy.

(g) Arvind Virmani

According to Arvind Virmani demonetization is a useful technique to solve the problem of black money, but he also said that it need the deeper study to check the effectiveness of demonetization. Immediate effects of demonetization is negative impact in retail trade in goods and services. Currency for everyday transaction have to be replace soon (Uke, 2017).

Problems/Issues due to Demonetization

Formation of long winding queues in front of each bank as well as ATM's from morning to evening. A considerable hue and cry from the public for getting their money exchanged. Bank employees have to work for longer hours. People are unable to withdraw huge amount for the big occasions at their home. A few deaths were accounted resulted from stress of not getting money, ultimately due to demonetization of currency. Most of the cashless transactions are connected through internet which demand proper network that is still inadequate in some parts of India. Many illegal agents (Dalals) are emerged who are indulged in exchange of notes with a huge commission resulting in moral degradation.

Illiterate or less educated people are not so much aware about the cashless transactions. Lack of ATM's especially in rural areas creates big problem. As some newspapers as well as news channels reported that back door policy on its way at some places in some banks with the involvement of some bank officials. Even some bank employees are found to be guilt indulging in conversion of 'black money' to 'white money'. Routine work of the people has got badly affected due to this movement of government. Less educated or illiterate people may have to face security issues in case of providing information relevant to their financial instruments to get transactions done through others (Sunil, 2017).

Shortcomings of the Policy

It will surely bring the clear view of every transaction within the country and promote cashless transaction. This step will affect general people to some extent but for the benefit of future generation such decisions are inevitable. Even though the demonetization process affects the retailers in large scale those who are providing essential goods and service to the people. This analysis helps to know how and what ways the demonetization process affect the sellers, shop owners, street vendors, small and medium enterprises (Kokila. & Ushadevi, 2017).

According the paper of Sunil (2017), the following shortcomings are still prevailing after the introduction of policy:

- People need training to use cashless transactions.
- The queues in banks as well as ATM's are not so much reduced even after passing the 46 days of policy implementation.
- Routine work of citizens is still going to effect.
- Banks are not getting adequate money.
- Even government offices are not well equipped with cashless payment tools/machines.
- At various ATM's, money is not provided in routine and even no money at some ATM's (interval is dissatisfactory).
- E- Payment is getting momentum but still a long way to go.
- People are still unable to withdraw huge amount for the occasions at their home.
- Proper networking facility is creating obstacles in the way of cashless payment.
- Bank employees are burdened with workload showing disinterest in work (Sunil, 2017).

Measures adopted by Government

According the paper of Sunil (2017), "a lot of measures have been adopted by the honourable government for smoothening the way of demonetization policy. Some of such measures are as follows:

- As stated by our honourable finance minister Shri Arun Jately, adequate money has been provided to bank with existing as well as new issued notes to overcome the demand from people.
- In a very short period, the government has issued a new denomination note of Rupees 2000 and after that the new note of

existing denomination of Rupees 500 has been issued in a very short span of time.

- The government has well clarified that the old currency notes will be in operation at public services places such as hospitals, for railway and bus ticket payment, petrol pups etc. for a limited period and even toll tax was completed removed for a small period to smoothen the transport.
- Government is promoting the cashless transaction and in this direction, government has taken initiative with some incentives such as insurance, e- payment discount offers etc. and recently lucky winners for each week using e-payment.
- A limit on withdrawn of money has been imposed for a limited period whether it is through ATM's or banks so that every citizen could accomplish his/her basic requirements.
- Central government as well as state government has made efforts to make their offices cashless that deal with public.
- Security official has been provided as well as enhanced in each bank as well as ATM's wherever needed to avoid the violence.
- The government has put its very big efforts through PMJDY (Pradhan Mantri Jan Dhan Yojana) accounts so that every citizen could be connected to banking services and really this effort has been proving fruitful in the demonetization move.
- Government has fastened the process of making technical changes in the ATM's to fit it with the new notes.
- To overcome the commission agents as well as black money holders, security forces in civil as well as in dress and CID officials as well are on their way and results are impressive" (Sunil. 2017).

Chapter - 6

Effects of Demonetization

Demonetization is a generations' memorable experience and is going to be one of the economic events of our time. Its impact is felt by every Indian citizen. Demonetization affects the economy through the liquidity side. Demonetization technically is a liquidity shock; a sudden stop in terms of currency availability. It creates a situation where lack of currencies jams consumption, investment, production, employment etc. In this context, the exercise may produce following short term/long term/, consumption/ investment, welfare/growth impacts on Indian economy. The intensity of demonetization effects clearly depends upon the duration of the liquidity shocks (Kasthuri, 2017).

India's demonetization exercise is quite distinct from the global economic record, in that its joint confidentiality and unexpectedness amidst normal economic and political conditions. Demonetization in other nations has occurred in the context of hyperinflation, wars, political turmoil, or other extreme circumstances.

The demonetisation, by removing 86 per cent of the currency in circulation, has resulted in a very severe contraction in money supply in the economy. This contraction, by wiping out cash balances in the economy, will eliminate a number of transactions for a while, since there is no or not enough of a medium of exchange available. In terms of the sectors in the economy, the sectors to be adversely affected are all those sectors where demand is usually backed by cash, especially those not within the organised retailing. For instance, transport services, kirana, fruits and vegetables and all other perishables, would face compression in demand which is backed by purchasing power. A further impact would be a compression of the demand for non-essentials by all the agents in the economy in the face of uncertainty in the availability of cash. The demand from segments which have access to digital medium of exchange would remain unaffected, but that from the rest of the economy would get compressed.

Another sector where one expects to see effects in the very short run is the real estate space. With contraction in demand from one set of agents – say agents who have earned unaccounted incomes and placed them within the real estate space – either prices within this segment would fall or transactions would cease to happen. The short-term effect on the economy would depend on the speed with which and the extent to which the cash is replaced by the authorities. Most of the purchases and sales in Rabi crop segment of the economy are carried out through cash. With the elimination of cash from the economy, sale of kharif crop would be difficult unless the crop is sold on the promise of payment in future. The second sector which could be adversely affected would be the construction sector. The sector, it is often argued, works with a significant amount of cash. Payments to workers as well as a variety of purchases might be carried out in cash. So, on the supply side, this sector can be adversely affected. On the other hand, on the demand side, the demand for houses and buildings would appear as a demand for non-essentials and might be pushed on to the back burner until the economic situation normalises.

For transactions to be restored to the pre-change level, a number of agents who are using cash as a medium of exchange have to move to using digital versions of money as the medium of exchange. There is growing literature that points out to the possibility of changes in spending behaviour as a result of moving to instruments other than cash. There are many substitutes for cash in the modern economy ranging from cheques, debit cards, pre-paid cards, credit cards and mobile wallets. When compared to cash, these instruments differ in a number of key characteristics.

Table 6.1. Dual Dimensions of Cash

Origin/Nature		
Function	**White**	**Black**
Transactions	Company pays employee salary in cash; payment and receipt are declared to tax authorities.	Small enterprise pays for input in cash; neither declares the transaction to tax authorities.
Store of Value	Household keeps savings in cash for emergencies	Businessman hoards undeclared cash, with a view to distributing it to his candidate during elections.

Source: Economic Survey 2016-17, Government of India, p. 56.

India's economy is relatively cash-dependent, even taking account of the fact that it is a relatively poor country. Attempts to reduce the cash in an economy could have important long-term benefits in terms of reducing levels of corruption. Understanding the benefits and costs of demonetisation requires spelling out the analytics of demonetisation, which are rich and complicated.

Black Money in India

There comes a time in the history of a country's development when a need is felt for a strong and critical step. For years, this country has felt that corruption, black money and terrorism are festering sores, holding us back in the race towards development. It is the fight against all above problems. The main aim of demonetization is the country moves to legalise black money's shadow economy, change acculturation of corruption and pull foreign investment and improve India's financial and banking framework, as well as take about all of India in the direction of conventional banking system.

Table 6.2: Top 10 Largest Countries include in Black Money

Rank	*Country Name*	*Black Money in Billions USD*
1.	United States	625.63
2.	China	261.00
3.	Mexico	126.00
4.	Spain	124.06
5.	Italy	111.05
6.	Japan	109.84
7.	Canada	77.83
8.	India	68.59
9.	United Kingdom	61.96
10.	Russia	49.09

Source: http://www.countrydetail.com/top-10-countries-largest-black-markets-world/March 11, 2016.

The money accumulated in the hands of a very few people due to tax evasion, illegal business deals, crimes, etc., or in which proper banking channel is not used is called black money. Also known as the "underground economy" or "black economy" these black markets are most elusive places where the law has no grounds. In layman, it is an amount which has no records under RBI (Chaudhary et. al., 2017).

Table 6.3: Black Money and GDP

Sl. No.	*Year*	*Estimates of Black Money (INR Lakh Crore)*	*% of GDP*
1.	2012	10	10
2.	2013	28	30
3.	2014	6	6
4.	2015	7	6.4
5,	2016	30	31

Source:http://www.thehindu.com/business/Economy/indias-black-economy-shrinks-says-ambit/article8693777.ece

The above tables reveal that there are top 10 largest countries which, is include in black money and India's black money in comparison to GDP. The fake notes are used for anti-national and illegal activities. High denomination notes have been misused by terrorists and for hoarding black money. India remains a cash-based economy; hence, the circulation of fake Indian currency notes continues to be a menace.

Table 6.4: Indian Money in Swiss Bank (in Swiss Francs)

Sl. No.	*Year*	*Indian money in Swiss Bank (in Swiss Francs)*	*Sl. No.*	*Year*	*Indian money in Swiss Bank (in Swiss Francs)*
1.	1996	1,219,270	11.	2006	4,987,822
2.	1997	1,645,899	12.	2007	2,923,209
3.	1998	1,755,948	13.	2008	1,585,004
4.	1999	1,994,423	14.	2009	1,391,268
5.	2000	1,509,321	15.	2010	1,657,736
6.	2001	1,950,674	16.	2011	2,025,072
7.	2002	1,847,011	17.	2012	1,344,162
8.	2003	2,205,132	18.	2013	1,952,712
9.	2004	3,961,827	19.	2014	1,776,099
10.	2005	4,197,215	20.	2015	1,206,709

Source: Chaudhary et. al. (2017). Demonetization: Experiment Mean of Financial Inclusion, International Journal of Innovative Studies in Sociology and Humanities, Volume: 2, Issue: 2, p. 4.

The above table reveals that how much Indian money deposited in Swiss Bank in Swiss Franc. 1,195 Indians have bank accounts registered in their names in the HSBC Geneva branch, according to a news report by Times of India, dated 9th February, 2015. Rs 4,479 crore is held in the accounts owned by Indians, who figured on the HSBC List, and the Income Tax Department has initiated action against 79 of such account holders. The term 'Black Money' evoke up images of untouchable Swiss bank accounts in the Indian visions. Some of this black money ends up in illicit financial flows across international borders, such as deposits in Swiss accounts.

As per the latest annual update on Swiss banks, released by Switzerland's central bank SNB (Swiss National Bank), the total money held there by foreign clients from across the world fell by nearly four per cent to Swiss franc 1.42 trillion (about Rs 98 lakh crore) at the end of 2015. In Swiss Bank many Indians have personal accounts in which $1,500 billion deposit in the form of foreign reserve which have been misappropriated, an amount 13 times larger than the country's foreign debt. With this amount 45 crore poor people can get Rs 1, 00,000 each (Chaudhary et. al., 2017).

Effects of Demonetization

Demonetization of currency is an excellent decision to stop corruption, and black money that doesn't re-enter the organization. This rigorous decision control and decimate major illegal activities such as corruption, terrorism, hoarding, fake currency and black money. Illegal weapons, intelligence and terrorist associated activities will be gag drastically due to lack of money.

Table 6.5. Impact of Demonetisation

Sector	*Effect through end-December*	*Likely longer-term effect*
Money/interest rates	Cash declined sharply. Bank deposits increased sharply. RBI's balance sheet largely unchanged: return of currency reduced the central bank's cash liabilities but increased its deposit liabilities to commercial banks. Interest rates on deposits, loans, and government securities declined; implicit rate on cash increased.	Cash will recover but settle at a lower level. Deposits will decline, but probably settle at a slightly higher level. RBI's balance sheet will shrink, after the deadline for redeeming outstanding notes. Loan rates could fall further, if much of the deposit increase proves durable.
Financial System Savings	Increased	Increase, to the extent that the cash deposit ratio falls permanently.
Corruption (underlying illicit activities)		Could decline, if incentives for compliance improve
Unaccounted income/black money (underlying activity may or may not be illicit)	Stock of black money fell, as some holders came into the tax net.	Formalization should reduce the flow of unaccounted income.
Private Wealth	Private sector wealth declined, since some high denomination notes were not returned and real estate prices fell.	Wealth could fall further, if real estate prices continue to decline.
Public Sector Wealth	No effect.	Government/RBI's wealth will increase when unreturned cash is extinguished, reducing liabilities.
Formalization/ digitilisation	Digital transactions amongst new users (RuPay/ AEPS) increased sharply; existing users' transactions increased in line with historical trend.	Some return to cash as supply normalises, but the now-launched digital revolution will continue.

(*Contd...*)

Real estate	Prices declined, as wealth fell while cash shortages impeded transactions.	Prices could fall further as investing undeclared income in real estate becomes more difficult; but tax component could rise, especially if GST imposed on real estate.
Broader economy	Job losses, decline in farm incomes, social disruption, especially in cash-intensive sectors.	Should gradually stabilize as the economy is remonetized
Gross domestic product	Growth slowed, as demonetisation reduced demand (cash, private wealth), supply (reduced liquidity and working capital, and disrupted supply chains), and increased uncertainty. Cash-intensive sectors (agriculture, real estate, jewellery) were affected more Recorded GDP will understate impact on informal sector because informal manufacturing is estimated using formal sector indicators (Index of Industrial Production). But over time as the economy becomes more formalized the underestimation will decline. Recorded GDP will also be overstated because banking sector value added is based (inter alia) on deposits which have surged temporarily.	Could be beneficial in the long run if formalization increases and corruption falls. Informal output could decline but recorded GDP would increase as the economy becomes more formalized.
Tax collection	Income taxes rose because of increased disclosure. Payments to local bodies and discoms increased because demonetised notes remained legal tender for tax payments/ clearances of arrears.	Indirect and corporate taxes could decline, to the extent growth slows. Over long run, taxes should increase as formalization expands and compliance improves.
Uncertainty/ Credibility	Uncertainty increased, as firms and households were unsure of the economic impact and implications for future policy Investment decisions and durable goods purchases postponed.	Credibility will be strengthened if demonetisation is accompanied by complementary measures. Early and full remonetisation essential. Tax arbitrariness and harassment could attenuate credibility

Source: Economic Survey 2016-17, Govt. of India, pp. 59-60.

Reports have also surfaced of the effects of demonetisation on human trafficking. A report in the UK's Guardian newspaper indicates that demonetisation complicated every point in the supply chain: suppliers had less capital to buy and transport people, from such states as Jharkhand, Assam and Bihar, and potential buyers were unable to pay for services. After the announcement of 8 November, it quickly became apparent that the banks were unprepared for the transition, owing to the unavailability of the new notes. Initially the amount of defunct currency that could be exchanged over the counter at banks was set at 4,000 Rupees; five days later this was increased to 4,500 Rupees; in late November 2016 over-the-counter exchanges ceased altogether.

At present there are no reliable figures on the cost of demonetisation to the economy; it has, however, had a major impact on the labour market, and has resulted in increased uncertainty and a fall in employment elasticity. The historic step taken by the Central Government, demonetizing more than two-thirds of the legal currency notes in circulation has put the entire economy in a state of confusion. Businesses across verticals are faced with testing times with the resulted stagnancy in cash transactions.

This move by the government is likely to have long term benefits for the economy. The extinguishing of the major proportion of unaccounted currency would reduce from the liabilities of the government and. would add to its finances. The move is also likely to have a habit changing impact in the Indian populous and there could be increased belief of keeping cash in the banks rather than stashed at home and use formal banking channels for their spending needs. With a large part of the cash moving through the banking channels, the banking sector is likely to be flush with funds in the near term and this would help them reduce cost of funds for such period.

Another element of the demonetization would be reduction in cash transactions in real estate. This is likely to reduce to real estate prices and make it affordable to some extent. This may be visible more in the rural belt, where many non-farming entities purchase fertile farmland, not for farming but for money parking purpose. This move is likely to lead to better tax compliance, raise the Tax to GDP ratio and improved tax collection. This could lead to lower borrowing and better fiscal management. Also with lower cash transactions in the near term, inflation may see downtrend in the near term (Source: HDFC Bank Investment Advisory Group).

Demonetisation clearly has had an immediate impact on many areas of the economy. The media reported anecdotally on the issues in diverse scenarios, which might be summarized by this vignette on the Forbes website: "Businesses shut down, farmers couldn't buy seeds, taxi and rickshaw drivers didn't have any way to receive payments, employers had no way to pay their employees, hospitals were refusing patients who only had old banknotes, fishermen watched their catch wither up and rot, some families had difficulty buying food, and weddings throughout the country were cancelled."

The expected and clearest short term impact on IT Trade and Business due to demonetization is the slump in hardware sales from cash transactions. Estimates for GDP growth have been reduced from 7.3 per cent to 5.8 per cent due to the perceived impact of monetization. "Cash shortage resulted in fewer new business intakes, which in turn caused a fall in activity and ended a 16-month sequence of expansion. All in all, IT and mobility are expected to be stable businesses. through national distribution, however, cash businesses trading in processors, memory storage and flash products would be hit. The long term impact on IT Industry, trade and business channels seems to be all positive. The move is expected to result in faster GDP growth, inflation is expected to dip, and products will become more affordable which will fuel the demand and further growth of industries.

The industries are expected to benefit since liquidity will come directly into the banks, leading to a rate reduction and hence more cash will flow into the market as part of loan. This is expected to create a positive impact on corporates who will be able to leverage more liquidity for newer projects and investment. As demonetization is predicted to lead to an increase in cash flow among banking institutions, business investment and expansion is set to thrive. Boon for IT businesses, as achieving a cashless economy, and emerging from the effects of demonetization requires massive digitization and IT deployment across enterprises as well as public organizations and consumers. In time, as things normalize, the bold move should accelerate economic growth through digital pipes of e-commerce and m-banking. It should result in the availability of larger revenues to the Government to fund infrastructure growth and the country wide internet penetration and digitization.

According to the Economic Survey 2016-17, Govt. of India report the benefits of demonetization are as below:

- **Tax on Black Money**

Demonetisation is as a tax administration measure. Accordingly, the scheme included a screening mechanism, aimed separating "white" income from "black". Cash holdings arising from income that had been declared could readily be deposited at banks and ultimately exchanged for new note. Those with black money faced three difficult choices. They could: (a) declare their unaccounted wealth and pay taxes at a penalty rate; (b) continue to hide it, not converting their old notes and thereby suffering a tax rate of 100 per cent; or, (c) launder their black money, paying a cost for converting the money into white. Other schemes would have required black money holders to pay a per centage to private intermediaries as a price for converting it into white.

In all these cases, black money holders still suffered a substantial loss, in taxes or "conversion fees". The December, 30, 2016 Ordinance has declared the unreturned notes as no longer constituting legal tender. When the grace period expires, the RBI could declare that these unreturned notes are no longer valid in any way, either as legal tender or as assets that can be exchanged for new currency.

- **Informal Sector**

Demonetisation has clearly had a detrimental effect on the income of casual labourers in the tertiary sector, who not only live their lives outside of the formal economy, but rely on cash for their income payments, and carry out virtually all of their transactions in cash. They constitute 92 per cent of the country's workforce and account for 59 per cent of India's GDP.

- **Tax compliance**

Demonetisation can be interpreted as a regime shift on the part of the government. It is a demonstration of the state's resolve to crack down on black money, showing that tax evasion will no longer be tolerated or accepted as an inevitable part of life. These two sanctions – financial penalty and social condemnation – could have a powerful and long-lasting effect on behaviour, especially if they were combined with other incentive-compatible measure. Demonetisation could also aid tax administration in another way, by shifting transactions out of the cash economy and into the formal payments system.

- **Effect on Price**

Price level is expected to be lowered due to moderation from demand side. This demand driven fall in prices could be understood as follows: (a) Consumer goods: Prices are expected to fall only marginally due to moderation in demand as use of cards and cheques would compensate for some purchases. (b) Real Estate and Property: Prices in this sector are largely expected to fall, especially for sales of properties where major part of the transaction is cash based, rather than based on banks transfer or cheque transactions. In the medium term, however the prices in this sector could regain some levels as developers rebalance their prices (probably charging more on cheque payment) (Sabnavis et. al., 2016).

• Tax on informal savings

Beyond reducing tax evasion, demonetisation could have other far-reaching effects. For example, it will channel savings into the formal financial system. In the longer-term, if demonetisation is successful, it will reduce the equilibrium cash-GDP and cash-deposits ratio in the economy. This will increase financial savings which could have a positive impact on long run growth.

• Digitalisation

One intermediate objective of demonetisation is to create a less-cash or cash-lite economy, as this is key to channelling more saving channelled through the formal financial system and improving tax compliance. According to Pricewaterhouse Coopers (2015) India has a very high predominance of consumer transactions carried out in cash relative to other countries. There are many reasons for this situation. Cash has many advantages: it is convenient, accepted everywhere, and its use is costless for ordinary people, though not of course for society at large. Cash transactions are also anonymous, helping to preserve privacy.

Digitalisation can broadly impact three sections of society: the poor, who are largely outside the digital economy; the less affluent, who are becoming part of the digital economy having acquired Jan Dhan accounts and RuPay cards; and the affluent, who are fully digitally integrated via credit cards. In the wake of the demonetisation, the government has taken a number of steps to facilitate and incentivize the move to a digital economy. Launch of the Bharat Interface for Money app for smartphones. This is based on the new Unified Payments Interface which has created inter-operability of digital transactions. So far, facilities such as RuPay and payment wallets still make up only a tiny proportion of digital transactions, much less overall financial transaction.

The impact on the digitally excluded category can be gleaned via transactions in the Aadhaar-Enabled Payments System. The impact on the middle category of digitally connected can be gleaned via Rupay transactions. As people have started to use such e-payment systems, they have discovered that it is more convenient to conduct financial activities electronically.

• Real estate

Demonetisation could have particularly profound impact on the real estate sector. In the past, much of the black money accumulated was ultimately used to evade taxes on property sales. To the extent that black money is reduced and financial transactions increasingly take place through electronic means, this type of tax evasion will also diminish. During November December 2016, the monthly average housing sales fell about 40 per cent in the top nine cities like Gurgaon, Ahmadabad, Kolkata, Chennai, Hyderabad, Bengaluru, Pune, Mumbai and Noida. Before demonetization the monthly average house sales was 19000 units in July month and 18000 units in October month (Uke, 2017).

- **Supply-side effects**

Demonetisation could also affect supplies of certain agricultural products, especially milk (where procurement has been low), sugar (where cane availability and drought in the Southern states will restrict production), and potatoes and onions (where sowings have been low). Vigilance is essential to prevent other agricultural products becoming in 2017-18 what pulses was in 2015-16 in terms of supply deficiencies and consequential higher inflation.

- **Effect on Banks**

As directed by the Government, the 500 and 1000 Rupee notes which now cease to be legal tender are to be deposited or exchanged in banks (subject to certain limits). This will automatically lead to more amounts being deposited in Savings and Current Account of commercial banks. This in turn will enhance the liquidity position of the banks, which can be utilized further for lending purposes. However, to the extent that households have held on to these funds for emergency purposes, there would be withdrawals at the second stage (Sabnavis et. al., 2016).

- **Effect on Demand**

The overall demand is expected to be affected to an extent. The demand in following areas is to be impacted particularly, consumer goods, real estate and property, gold and luxury goods, and automobiles (only to a certain limit). All these mentioned sectors are expected to face certain moderation in demand from the consumer side, owing to the significant amount of cash transactions involved in these sectors (Sabnavis et. al., 2016).

- **Redistribute resources**

Demonetisation will also redistribute resources. For example, to the extent that black money holders have laundered their money by employing people to stand in queues there could be a positive wealth effect because cash would go from agents with a low propensity to spend to those with a greater propensity to spend (Source: Economic Survey 2016-17, Govt. of India).

- **FMCG industry**

FMCC industry had gone down by 1-1.5 per cent or Rs 3,840 crores in November, compared to October. The purchase in November had gone down by 6.4 per cent compared to October. Purchase of personal care items such as toilet soaps, toothpaste and shampoo had seen the greatest fall by retailers. According to consumer point of view, one out of five housewives had reduced spending by 50 per cent or more. They had cut spends across categories for impulse categories such as biscuits, salty snacks compared to everyday essentials like atta, rice, pulse, sugar(Uke, 2017).

- **Automobile Sector**

Indian auto industry attracts major global payers from all segments. Fiat, Volkswagen, Honda, Nissan, become the common brands seen on Indian roads. Increasing GDP has further lured them to expand product line in India. An indigenous player, Maruti Suzuki and Tata Motors has their share of market from passenger car segment. Indian car industry transactions are predominantly characterised by the cash transactions. With the growing industry and world's largest market for auto mobile product, it is important to study demonetisation impact on auto industry.

Indian Demonetisation has shaken the economy and lots of mix response has recorded, few industries are hoping to get positive impact whereas few fear to get hard hit. Automobile industry is one such which has negative impact. Sudden announcement of demonetisation has resulted into insecurity and fear among car buyers where major part is cash sales. The hatchback, sedan and SUV were the harder hit. Car industry lists into major industry contributing to economic wealth for country (Katke et. al., 2017).

- **Agricultural Sector**

Demonetisation has affected every Indian, but it has hit the agricultural sector badly. Agriculture in India accounts for 50 per cent of the workforce. Sale, transport, marketing and distribution of ready produce to mandis is dominantly cash-dependent. Farmers suffered a setback due to nationwide cash shortage and a fall in the demand for vegetables in wholesale markets. Farmers were not able to purchase inputs like seeds from market. They were using old seeds from the last year harvest and not purchasing new quality seeds from market. The consumers of rural farmer are not as advance as the urban middle class, which can be easily managed with a very little amount of cash. The problem of the demonetization is largely associated with the rural areas of the country have lesser number of banks and ATMs compared to the urban areas and semi-urban areas (Shah, 2017).

• Reduce Government Liability

It will reduce the risk and cost of cash handling as soft money is safer than hard money. It will also reduce government liability. Since every note is a liability for the government, the old currency will become worthless for those people, who choose not to disclose their income. Thus, this will extinguish government's liability to that extent. It is expected approximately Rs 5 lakh crore may come to the government in the form of extinguished RBI liability, taxes and penalties. It will reduce tax avoidance (Shirley, 2017).

• Impact on counterfeit currency

The real impact will be on counterfeit/fake currency as its circulation will be checked after this exercise. It was previously estimated that 250 out of every million Indian bank notes were fakes. The new 500 and 2,000 rupee notes are less vulnerable to counterfeiting, having advanced security features with one report claiming that it will be "impossible" for Pakistan to fake them. The Demonetization has badly hit Maoist and Naxalites as well. The surrender rate has reached its highest since the demonetization is announced (Shirley, 2017).

• Hawala

The brightest spot is the end of Hawala racket and rising property prices. Hawala is the way of transferring money from a different country to India in Indian denominations. Although illegal, the people in this racket make their money white through this process in different countries. To attract more people to remit through this form, they pay a premium over the existing exchange rates mostlyfor remitters from African based nations. Come 8th November, 2016, the government scrapped all high denominations making the notes lying with the Hawala traders null and void (Shirley, 2017).

Impact of Demonetization on FMCG sector

According Kaur & Kaur (2017), Fast Moving Consumer Goods is also known as consumer packaged goods. Items in this category include all consumables (other than groceries/pulses) people buy at regular intervals. The most common in the list are toilet soaps, detergents, shampoos, toothpaste, shaving products, shoe polish, packaged foodstuff, and household accessories and extends to certain electronic goods (cells). These items are meant for daily or frequent consumption and have a high return. Rural areas expected to be the major driver for FMCG, as growth continues to be high in these regions. Rural areas saw a 16 per cent, as against 12 per cent rise in urban areas. Most companies rushed to capitalise on this, as they quickly went about increasing direct distribution and providing better infrastructure. Companies are also working towards creating specific products specially targeted for the rural market.

The Government of India has also been supporting the rural population with higher minimum support prices, loan waivers, and disbursements through the National Rural Employment Guarantee Act programme. These measures have helped in reducing poverty in rural India and given a boost to rural purchasing power. With rise in purchasing power, mid- and high-income consumers in urban areas have shifted their purchasing trend from essential to premium products.

In FMCG Industry, more than 80-85 per cent transactions between retailers to distributors are cash based. Further though most of the large FMCG companies do not extend credit to distributors, but distributors tend to extend credit to retailers typically for a period ranging between 7 days to 3 weeks. Under-reporting of sale at retailer level and transactions without bill by distributors is a rampant practice in trade and is something ignored by FMCG players being off book. Packaged Drinking Water and Carbonated soft drinks are the largest selling items (amongst packaged goods) in small restaurants. As per the National Restaurants Association of India, Consumer spends at restaurants have dropped as much as 40 per cent post the demonetization announcement, a clear indication of discretionary spends getting impacted by liquidity crunch.

The good thing which is expected to come out of this is the greater acceptance of digital payments systems which eventually will reduce cost of doing business at all levels (Manufacturer to Retailer). Retail chains such as Big Bazaar and Godrej Nature's Basket saw the biggest upswing due to the availability of card machines in their stores during the demonetization period. Paytm has been declared an official bank for wallet money. People who could never imagine transacting online or using mobile wallets are now making extensive use of the same. Even transporters are now heavily making use of Paytm for making various payments while they are on road (toll payments).

"Demonetization of high value currency note initiated by the government is a positive move for the economy and industry and will lead to better transparency and compliance in the medium to long run. This will be beneficial for organised FMCG players creating a level playing field," Dabur Ltd said a regulatory filing. Elaborating on the impact, the company said it will vary across channels and geographies and stress is highest for wholesalers and small town grocery shops, who are facing a severe liquidity crisis and are destocking.

Life is getting back to normal with change in withdrawals from ATMs per day, shorter ques at the ATMs, less pressure on the bankers, increased amount of cash in hand, people equipping to use digital methods of payments etc. As a positive effect of demonetization, there is a move towards formal economy and organised national players. It might be challenging for the regional players who are largely unorganized in nature. Sooner we adopt to varied means of transactions easier it will be to evade losses (Kaur & Kaur, 2017).

Deposits in Pradhan Mantri Jan Dhan Yojana Account

During Post-demonetisation, 23.3 million new accounts were opened under the Pradhan Mantri Jan Dhan Yojana (PMJDY), bulk of which (80 per cent) were with public sector banks. Of the new Jan Dhan accounts opened, 53.6 per cent were in urban areas and 46.4 per cent in rural areas. Deposits under PMJDY accounts increased significantly post demonetisation. The total balance in PMJDY deposit accounts peaked at 746 billion as on December 7, 2016 from 456 billion as on November 9, 2016 - an increase of 63.6 per cent. As there were reports regarding the use of these accounts to convert black money into white, the Government issued a warning against the misuse of such accounts.

Table 6.6: Deposits under PMJDY: Number of Accounts (in million)

<table>
<tr><th rowspan="2">Bank-Group</th><th colspan="3">As on November 9, 2016</th><th colspan="3">As on March 1, 2017</th><th colspan="3">Variation
(March 1, 2017 over November 9, 2016)</th></tr>
<tr><th>Rural</th><th>Urban</th><th>Total</th><th>Rural</th><th>Urban</th><th>Total</th><th>Rural</th><th>Urban</th><th>Total</th></tr>
<tr><td>Public Sector Banks</td><td>114.3</td><td>89.3</td><td>203.6</td><td>122.1</td><td>100.8</td><td>222.9</td><td>7.8
(6.8)</td><td>11.5
(12.9)</td><td>19.3
(9.5)</td></tr>
<tr><td>Regional Rural Banks</td><td>37.1</td><td>6.0</td><td>43.1</td><td>40.0</td><td>6.4</td><td>46.4</td><td>2.9
(7.8)</td><td>0.4
(6.8)</td><td>3.3
(7.7)</td></tr>
<tr><td>Private Sector Banks</td><td>5.3</td><td>3.1</td><td>8.4</td><td>5.4</td><td>3.6</td><td>9.0</td><td>0.1
(1.3)</td><td>0.5
(16.8)</td><td>0.6
(7.0)</td></tr>
<tr><td>Scheduled Commercial Banks</td><td>156.7</td><td>98.4</td><td>255.1</td><td>167.5</td><td>110.9</td><td>278.4</td><td>10.8
(6.9)</td><td>12.5
(12.7)</td><td>23.3
(9.1)</td></tr>
</table>

Source: Pradhan Mantri Jan Dhan Yojana website.

Table 6.7: Deposits Under PMJDY: Amount Mobilised (billion)

Bank Group	*As on November 9, 2016*	*As on March 1, 2017*	*Variation*	*Variation in aggregate deposits of scheduled commercial banks (February 17, 2017 over November 11, 2016*	*Accretion in PMJDY deposits as percentage of accretion in Aggregate deposits*
Public Sector Banks	364.0	502.5	138.5 (38.0)	2733.0 (3.9)	5.1
Regional Rural Banks	76.3	118.1	41.8 (55.0)	616.0 (18.0)	6.8
Private Sector Banks	16.0	22.3	6.3 (39.0)	778.0 (3.5)	0.8
Scheduled Commercial Banks	456.4	642.9	186.5 (41.0)	4098.0 (4.1)	4.6

Source: PradhanMantri Jan DhanYojana website.

The Government also capped deposits into PMJDY accounts at 50,000 on November 15, 2016. Although deposits declined to 643 billion as on March 1, 2017, they were still higher by 41 per cent over the level of November 9, 2016. As a huge increment can be seen in the deposits in the accounts opened under PMJDY which not only indicates that a huge amount of money has been deposited by the persons having colossal amount of cash in hand, into these accounts but it would also create a big problem for banks to utilise such funds in such a manner to get an effective return (Meher, 2017).

Post-Demonetization Effort

One of the aims of demonetisation was the acceleration of the digital economy. It is interesting to note that in November and December 2016, there was, according to the Reserve Bank of India a marked increase in digital payments – particularly point-of-sale (PoS) card transactions. There are various strictures on the future growth of digital payments, including the relative scarcity of PoS and ATM facilities; this is currently being addressed through a government mandate for the installation of new electronic facilities.

Another initiative undertaken in the wake of demonetisation is the roll-out of a Goods and Services Tax in September 2017. While the institution of this measure will have an adverse impact on the informal, rural, and cash-based sectors of the economy initially, it might have long-term structural benefits. The combined factors of demonetisation and GST could result in a wider tax base, and greater participation in the formal economy, which should benefit India's business climate and financial system.

Overall Impact of Demonetization

This bulk movement taken towards the melioration of Indian society have some major impacts on the economy of the country. Thus, here are some of the major effects of demonetization of Indian economy.

- Due to reserved transaction, circulation, and supply of money, there will be minor chances of continue black money by defaulters in our system and society.
- The weaker sections of the society who are not well open to technology and are not aware of cashless payment system, may find some difficulties in starting, but the overall impact is going to be positive for everyone in the long term.
- GDP growth is imagining being negative about 6 months.
- Inflation is imagining falling sharply with fall in Real Estate prices and transaction costs thereof. Inflation could decrease and deflation increase.
- Real Estate and Jewellery sectors, though hit initially will brace in few months.
- Government Deficit will immense boom in the next 2 years.
- This big step will cause low economic activity and bluntness in the consumption demand, but this drop will be remunerated in due course of time, and the system will be neat and svelte (Chaudhary et. al., 2017).

PART - III
CASHLESS ECONOMY

Chapter - 7

Cashless Economy

Cash is like water a basic necessity without which survival is a challenge. Nevertheless, cash use doesn't seem to be waning all that much, with around 85 per cent of global payments still made using cash. Cash provides individuals and families with liquidity. One needs not to worry about a computer system crashing, power going off, and losing transaction midway. Use of cash doesn't involve any extra cost as in the use of debit/credit cards (Tawade, 2017).

The 1990s also saw the entrance of technology in India and people were introduced with the use of personal computers and gradually the automation took every sector by storm and now we can see the virtual world that exists and anything can happen in it from uniting the world to initiate a war if not handled properly. Although there have been various initiatives taken by our Honourable Prime Minister Mr Narendar Modi such as Make in India, Swatch Bharat Abhiyan, Digital India etc. But it was during this money crunch when people started recognising the benefits of being digitally sound and how useful it is. Our government has emphasised ongoing cashless as it will make transactions smoother and transparent and eliminates the existence of parallel economy (Kual & Mathur, 2017).

Consider two truths about technology. First, technology only moves forward, each advance building on the last until an inevitable breakthrough changes everything. Second, technology is impartial in its impact— how each advance affects individuals and society is left in large part to political and social institutions to determine. Eras of rapid technological change, such as the industrial and information revolutions, delivered both widespread benefits and economic and social disruption. Digitalisation, which we define as the broad adoption of digital technology in homes, businesses and society, constitutes a transformative shift in technology across industries and society in general. It fundamentally changes the way people live, work and communicate and how they discover and purchase goods and services.

From shopping to entertainment to socialising to managing the household— and household finances—digital technologies have fundamentally altered human behavior and consumers that have been presented with the opportunity have been quick to integrate digital tools into their daily lives. Digital and mobile technologies have transformed the customer experience in payments and banking. Digital technology and the economic activity that it enables deliver broad economic and social benefits. The experiences of very different markets around the world—China, India, South Korea, Sweden and the US, for example—show that digital economies can take root and grow under all kinds of circumstances, if a few basic factors are in place. A good telecommunications infrastructure is the prerequisite for digital inclusion and for a strong and growing digital economy.

What is Cashless Economy?

Cashless Economy can be defined as a situation in which the flow of cash within an economy is non-existent and all transactions must be through electronic channels such as direct debit, credit cards, debit cards, electronic clearing, and payment systems such as Immediate Payment Service, National Electronic Funds Transfer and Real Time Gross Settlement in India (Tawade, 2017).

A cashless society describes an economic state whereby financial transactions are not conducted with money in the form of physical banknotes or coins, but rather through the transfer of digital information (usually an electronic representation of money) between the transacting parties. The trend towards use of non-cash transactions and settlement began in daily life during the 1990s, when electronic banking became popular. By the 2010s digital payment methods were widespread in many countries, with examples including intermediaries such as PayPal, digital wallet systems operated by companies like Apple, contactless and NFC payments by electronic card or smartphone, and electronic bills and banking, all in widespread use.

Importance of Cashless Transactions

India is moving towards a digital revolution. The transition while drastic has been in cards for a long time now. Post demonetization, there has been a frenzy in the minds of the general public with regards to the whole digitization process. Once people get hang of the digital payment and transactions system, people are sure to become a fan of online shopping. One of the most lauded benefits of going cashless is the ease with which all the payment transactions can be performed. Deposit your cash into the bank and join the millions who are enjoying the ease of digital transactions using credit cards, debit cards, mobile wallets, UPI apps and USSD Banking.

Decision to adopt the digitization process and to go cashless can help enjoy many incentives, freebies, and discounts. While government themselves have announced a list of incentives for going cashless, one should not forget the offers, discounts, and cashbacks provided by various mobile wallet operators like PayTM, Mobikwik etc. The SMS trail after every transaction helps to keep a track of spending. A major benefit of going cashless would be to not worry about the odd change. The beauty of cashless transactions is that you can make the exact payment to the last paisa, be it 0.90 Rs or 0.01 Rs

When any person indulges in cashless payments for spending's, that person are constantly reminded of the available bank balance after each transaction. This constant reminder will help refrain from spending on unnecessary items and thus help stay within budget. Cash once stolen hardly ever comes back. The money is lost forever. But if get robbed of debit or credit cards, that can easily block them remotely and be assured that will face no loss of money. That is a major plus of going cashless. If people decide to adopt financial digitization, then need not worry about the counterfeit currency at all. The debit cards and credit cards cannot be counterfeited and thus going cashless keeps people away from the hassles of handling counterfeit currency.

More people joining the cashless revolution would mean reduction in the volume of paper money to be produced. This would definitely help the environment and our surroundings as less paper requirement would mean lesser trees being cut. In today's term, a cashless society is described as an economic state whereby financial transactions are not conducted with money in physical form (banknotes or coins) but rather through the transfer of digital information. Advocates saw the potential in digital transactions as it allows for quicker transactions regardless of location and not limited by time which empowers individuals with access to financial services.

According to Government of India the cashless policy will increase employment, reduce cash related robbery thereby reducing risk of carrying cash. Cashless policy will also reduce cash related corruption and attract more foreign investors to the country. In many countries introduction of cashless economy can be seen as steps in the right direction. It is expected that its impact will be felt in modernization of payment system, Reduction in the cost of banking service, Reduction in high security and safety risk and also curb banking related corruption (Thilagavathy& Santhi, 2017).

So according Shendge et. al. (2017), “the importance of Cashless Transactions is:

- Taxation: with lesser availability of hard cash at homes and more in banks, there is lesser scope of hiding income and evading taxation and when there are more tax payers it ultimately leads to a lesser rate of taxation for the whole country.
- Transparency and accountability: it becomes a lot easier to track the flow of money with every transaction being recorded with the buyer, seller as well as regulatory bodies, making the system much more transparent and compliant. In the long term it leads to better business and investment prospects for the economy as a whole.
- Reduced red tapism and bureaucracy: with cashless transactions through electronic means the wire transfers are tracked and people are accountable which in turn reduces corruption and improves service time.
- The exact amount in small denominations can be paid. Unlike cash transactions, there is no need to pay fringe amount in case the exact amount is not available with either of the parties. An important, though seemingly insignificant issue is that of hygiene of the notes.
- Tracking of expenses: it becomes easier to determine how much was spent where.
- No fear of being robbed unlike carrying cash and letting everyone know that there could be something worth snatching.
- Less availability of cash for illegal activities: when people are encouraged to go cashless, there is lesser cash available with the people and there won’t be a means to invest in other activities to use the idle cash. Channels like hawala (illegal remittance) will ultimately suffer the brunt of a cashless economy.

- Pack of cards: No need to carry bulky notes in a case. Just carrying the required cards or mobile banking will suffice. More sense of safety with a PIN protected card etc. which will work only with your own credentials."

Current Position of Cashless India

India's black money has been estimated by the World Bank in 2010 to be worth about one fifth of the GDP. In a country where 90 per cent transactions are carried out on cash basis it was a revolutionary move to transform from cash to cashless transactions. To bring the economy on track again, government is promoting cashless economy because scrapping of cash needs an alternative to cash. Under this scheme, 250 million bank accounts have been opened in two years. As per RBI reports bank branches increased by five per cent per year but ATMs, debit cards and card swiping machines have doubled in four years and online transactions have grown 20 times in six years to 2016. The whole country is witnessing the effects of demonetization and with our Prime Minister hinting at a cashless economy, many people are left in confusion. How would a cashless economy be beneficial is the question of man (Tawade, 2017).

On the 126th birth ceremony of B. R. Ambedkar Prime Minister Narendra Modi made a new step towards Digital India. On this very occasion in Nagpur Modi has launched Aadhaar Pay using BHIM App. This app will allow consumers to pay with their biometric data, linked to their Aadhaar. This BHIM App is expected to reconstruct the way of digital marketing, particularly in rural India. This new payment method is named as the BHIM Aadhaar Sewa by the government.

Government of India is encouraging people to move towards a Cashless Economy. Cashless Economy can be achieved when the use of cash within the economy is gradually reduced and all transactions are made through electronic medium as well as through cheques.

Advantages of Cashless Payments

Companies and governments will get efficient and they can reduce costs as they no longer need the manual accounting work to be done. The costs associated with accounting and handling cash is very high. Production of coins and paper currency is indeed an expensive endeavour and the life span of most of the paper currencies is about 6 years. So, by going electronic the cost of production gets reduced. The government can use the data coming from the cashless transactions to improve and analyse their policies. By using such data, officials can predict or identify the patterns of activity and use such information for urban planning for sectors like energy management, housing, and transportation. In addition to this, going cashless also has health benefits. With physical currency, the chance of spreading of germs is more. Reducing the amount of use of paper currency will reduce the germ transmission (Tawade, 2017).

Going digital, it helps to reduce the hassle of drawing cash or making sure that cash-in-hand is sufficient to make a payment in places where only cash payment is allowed. With a digitalized payment system, it speeds up the process of financial transaction and boosts the efficiency of the transaction. As monetary transactions are being made electronically, it increases the transparency as financial transaction are recorded. Cashless payments would eliminate the fear of businesses receiving counterfeit money and flush out illegal cash. The risks of storing cash will also be reduced as payments are made digitally. As digital payments are made, transactions are kept in records. Cashless payments facilitate the tracking of spending expenditure and record the movement of money. Having recorded transactions, it can help citizens to refine their budget more efficiently (Cashless society, 2018).

According Gaur & Padiya (2017), the cashless transactions provide benefit in long run and it changes the deep-rooted behaviour among the people.

- Cost Effective to Banks: If a transaction is done manually at the branch of the bank it costs Rs 40 to 45 but if the same transaction is done through online it costs roughly Rs 7 to 8. This reduces the cost of operation for the banks and also makes it convenient for both banker and the customer.
- Low Time Consumption: Apparently, the cashless transactions reduce the time consumption for the customers and it minimizes the count of customer complaints. The customers, with the help of various options for cashless transactions, transfer or receive the amount in a matter of minutes and saves the time of visiting and carrying out the transactions in the bank branch.
- Safe and Secure: Cashless transactions provide high-end security by means of availing the facility of fingerprints and One Time Password (OTP) for every transaction.
- Up-gradation of Technology: The shift from the conventional banking to cashless transactions brings technological advancement.

The banks increase their ATMs, PoS machines count and various other features in the e-banking domain periodically.

- Control of Black Money and Check for Anti-Money Laundry: There is a traceability feature in e-banking unlike the cash transaction so it is easy to check the anti-money laundry and black money circulation in the country. It reduces many financial scams in our country and enhances the proper economic growth (Gaur & Padiya, 2017).

Impact of Cashless Transaction

According Shendge et. al. (2017), the impact of cashless transactions are:

(a) Business Process

The impacts of Cashless Transaction on the Business sector are as following: (a) Businesses are legally strong. (b) Proper audit. Not hidden excess liability. (c) Increase use of e-payment. (d) Wallet hold business gets an advantage.

(b) Education Process

The impact of Cashless Transaction on the education sector is likely to be minimal. Some of the foreseeable fallouts of demonetization on the Indian education sector are as following:

- The decision of the central government to withdraw high-value bank notes to curb unaccounted cash will hurt education institutions that accept donations or capitation fees for admissions.
- Accepting and accounting donations will become difficult because of the demonetisation drive. Education sector was not immune to the Indian theory of 'you can buy everything with money'. This move of demonetisation will definitely curb this mentality of many in the country.
- Private educational institutions take huge of amount of donations in Cash which is 40 per cent to 50 per cent more than the fees of the course. We expect that demonetisation will impact the recipient.
- Admissions in private educational institutions and medical college admissions comes tagged along with donations without a glitch. The donations in medical colleges is usually more than 100 per cent of the fees. Demonetisation will impact both admissions and also the receipt.

- MBBS seats is some colleges goes for Rs 40 lakh to Rs 60 lakh, while MD seats has a range of Rs 2 crore price tag on it. Similarly, engineering and management stream seats have a price tag between Rs 2 lakh to Rs 10 lakh each. This move can change the course of expensive education which can be made more affordable devoid of the capitation fee.

(c) Economic Growth

The impact of Cashless Transaction on Economic Growth in India is as following: (a) According to the Bank, India's growth in the first half of FY 2017 was underpinned by robust private and public consumption, which offset slowing fixed investment, subdued industrial activity and lethargic exports, and (b) The medium-term may be liquidity expansion in the banking system, helping to lower lending rates and lift economic activity," the World Bank noted.

(d) Impact of Information Technology in cashless economy

The impact of Information Technology on in cashless economy in India is as following:

- Because of information technology the cost of bank will reduce that will result in lower service charges for customers.
- Making Transaction is very easy by using information technology.
- New IT Technology like biometric are help to do secure and transparent transaction (Shendge et. al., 2017).

Digital Currency

Digital currency (digital money or electronic money or electronic currency) is a type of currency available only in digital form, not in physical (such as banknotes and coins). It exhibits properties similar to physical currencies, but allows for instantaneous transactions and borderless transfer-of-ownership. Digital currency is a money balance recorded electronically on a stored-value card or other device. Another form of electronic money is network money, allowing the transfer of value on computer networks, particularly the Internet (Digital currency, 2018).

Disadvantages of Cashless Payments

The main problem may be cybercrime. Computer fraud are happening in many parts of India. ATM pin number, card number, CVV number all should be keep secret by the people. Many times hackers can withdraw money from one account or online transfer by collecting that information's from the account holder or cardholder. Unknown call to the cardholder regarding ATM pin number, card number, CVV number of debit card/credit card is common now-a-days. There are many incidence of transfer money from account by hackers. So people have fear whether such information is leaked to any person or not.

According Tawade (2017), since the day demonetisation was announced, people are trying to use more of card transactions to save that dreaded trip to the bank and to save the last penny of the hard cash in hand. However, a sudden surge in card transactions has led to connectivity issues. Several people have faced trouble while standing in line to pay for a transaction at a shop when the card machines have stopped working due to an overload on the network.

Internet connectivity is needed even for the e-wallets. In order to convince people to do cashless transactions, the cost of the internet should be lowered and free WiFi should also be provided at public places. Not many people are comfortable using computers or mobile phones and depend on their children when it comes to using the gizmos. So literacy among people for using mobile or ATM machine is important. Several companies have come up with new and inexpensive phones, but they still not affordable for most of the population in the country. More affordable options should be launched by the government for people to buy smartphones for cashless transactions.

A cashless society needs a proper infrastructure. The banks need to be fully equipped to handle the surge in e-transactions. Infrastructure is also needed in terms of opening more accounts in the banks. Most people still do not have bank accounts. Most often there is just one account per family which also limits the number of cards people can have individually. A family of even four people cannot be dependent on just one card for all household expenditure. A cashless society is a welcome idea but not without preparation. There is a precursor to taking such steps without which a move such as this would be more harmful that being beneficial (Tawade, 2017).

Digitalization and Demonetization

According the paper of Kaul & Mathur (2017), "Digitalization transition through Digital India Programme aims to provide the much needed thrust to the nine pillars of growth areas, namely Broadband Highways, Universal Access to Mobile Connectivity Public Internet Access Programme, e-Governance: Reforming Government through Technology, eKranti -

Electronic Delivery of Services, Information for All, Electronics Manufacturing, IT for Jobs and Early Harvest Programmes. Every pillar has its own importance, complexities in implementation and is a propellant for the overall growth of the country.

- Broadband Highways: It covers three components broadband for all rural, broadband for all urban and National information infrastructures.
- Universal Access to Mobile Connectivity: It focuses on network penetration and filling the gaps in connectivity in the country.
- Public Internet Access Programme: To provide Common Services Centres (CSCs) and Post Offices as multi-service centres.
- e-Governance: Reforming Government through Technology: Government Process Reengineering using IT to simplify and make the government processes more efficient is critical for transformation to make the delivery of government services more effective across various government domains and therefore needs to be implemented by all Ministries/ Departments.
- e-Kranti: Electronic Delivery of Services: The Government approved the National eGovernance Plan (NeGP), comprising of 31 Mission Mode Projects (MMPs) and 8 components. e-Kranti is an essential pillar of the Digital India initiative and there are 44 Mission Mode Projects under e-Kranti, which are at various stages of implementation. (includes Banking, Post office, Income tax, Land records, Agriculture, Gram Panchayats etc.
- Information for All: Online hosting of information & documents to facilitate open and easy access to information for citizens.
- Electronics Manufacturing: It focuses on promoting electronics manufacturing in the country with the target of NET ZERO Imports by 2020 as a striking demonstration of intent.
- IT for Jobs: It focuses on providing training to the youth in the skills required for availing employment opportunities in the IT/ ITES sector.
- Early Harvest Programmes: It consists of those projects which are to be implemented within short timeline (Kaul & Mathur, 2017)."

Digitalization and GDP Growth

Impact of digitalization on a country can be assessed on the basis of its impact on the government, on the economy and the society. The digitalization has created new job opportunities, have led to innovation in very sector and also led to the growth of the economy i.e. have helped in the GDP growth of the country. The government has emphasised on the digitalization as it brings transparency, better control, better job opportunities, it also provides an ease of access to the people and an upward movement in their quality of life.

India is known as the powerhouse of the software industry and is in a leading position in global sourcing market but there is still a great deal of work to done for its Digital India campaign. Digitalization will be helpful if it can reach the maximum people and for that each and every citizen of the country should be able to easily access the facilities. India has also started collaborating with various countries and business organizations (like Google, Cisco etc.) for speeding up its digitalization process by infrastructural development, increasing access to internet and also started the transformation of cities to smart city (Kaul & Mathur, 2017).

Obstacles in the Process of Digitalization

- The resistance to change people show during emergence of new technology.
- Building trust among the people for change is difficult.
- Lack of knowledge about its use and benefits.
- Infrastructure requirements and their unavailability also hamper the reaching of these basic facilities to the people.
- The basic hindrance is the lack of literacy and literacy is not just to be able to write one's name and do the signature but to have an understanding of the changes going in the technology, society and the country for their own betterment (Kaul & Mathur, 2017).

Digital India Programme

The Digital India programme is a flagship programme of the Government of India with a vision to transform India into a digitally empowered society and knowledge economy. "Faceless, Paperless, Cashless" is one of professed role of Digital India.

According the website of Cashless India, various modes of digital payments are:

- Banking cards offer consumers more security, convenience, and control than any other payment method. The wide variety of cards available – including credit, debit and prepaid – offers enormous flexibility, as well. These cards provide 2 factor authentication for secure payments e.g secure PIN and OTP. RuPay, Visa, MasterCard are some of the example of card payment systems.

- Unstructured Supplementary Service Data (USSD) channel. service allows mobile banking transactions using basic feature mobile phone, there is no need to have mobile internet data facility for using USSD based mobile banking. It is envisioned to provide financial deepening and inclusion of underbanked society in the mainstream banking services.
- Micro ATM meant to be a device that is used by a million Business Correspondents (BC) to deliver basic banking services. The platform will enable Business Correspondents to conduct instant transactions. The micro platform will enable function through low cost devices (micro ATMs) that will be connected to banks across the country. Customers would just have to get their identity authenticated and withdraw or put money into their bank accounts. This money will come from the cash drawer of the BC.
- Mobile banking is a service provided by a bank or other financial institution that allows its customers to conduct different types of financial transactions remotely using a mobile device such as a mobile phone or tablet. It uses software, usually called an app, provided by the banks or financial institution for the purpose.
- Internet banking, also known as online banking, e-banking or virtual banking, is an electronic payment system that enables customers of a bank or other financial institution to conduct a range of financial transactions through the financial institution's website. National Electronic Funds Transfer is a nation-wide payment system facilitating one-to-one funds transfer. Real Time Gross Settlement is defined as the continuous (real-time) settlement of funds transfers individually on an order by order basis (without netting). Electronic Clearing System is an alternative method for effecting payment transactions in respect of the utility-bill-payments such as telephone bills, electricity bills, insurance premia, card payments and loan repayments, etc.,
- Immediate Payment Service offers an instant, 24X7, interbank electronic fund transfer service through mobile phones. IMPS is an emphatic tool to transfer money instantly within banks across India through mobile, internet and ATM which is not only safe but also economical both in financial and non-financial perspectives.

- A mobile wallet is a way to carry cash in digital format. An individual's account is required to be linked to the digital wallet to load money in it. Most banks have their e-wallets and some private companies. e.g. Paytm, Freecharge, Mobikwik, Oxigen, mRuppee, Airtel Money, Jio Money, SBI Buddy, itz Cash, Citrus Pay, Vodafone M-Pesa, Axis Bank Lime, ICICI Pockets, SpeedPay etc.
- Unified Payments Interface (UPI) is a system that powers multiple bank accounts into a single mobile application (of any participating bank), merging several banking features, seamless fund routing & merchant payments into one hood. It also caters to the "Peer to Peer" collect request which can be scheduled and paid as per requirement and convenience. Each Bank provides its own UPI App for Android, Windows and iOS mobile platform (Source: http://cashlessindia.gov.in/).

Trust, Safety and Security

Using digital services beyond basic search requires trust in the digital system: users must feel safe online, transactions must be secure and private, and goods ordered and paid for should be delivered. Without this trust, no digital economy can thrive. Safe, easy-to-use digital identities that serve multiple online purposes are a critical component of the security solution.

Multiple studies have concluded that digital ecosystems that produce local content and apps are vital for building digital literacy, attracting local users and serving local needs. Digital services can be a big step towards addressing local problems and boosting competition in an increasingly international digital services market.

The impact of digital technologies on business, especially small and medium-sized enterprises, has been transformative. There are virtually no industries today that do not apply digital technologies in some way in their product manufacturing, service provision, or business processes. Governments that use policy levers, from removing obstacles to facilitating adoption to incentivising digitalisation, can encourage more companies to digitalise their operations and expand the digital economy. The good news is that in many markets, the cost of the investment required to digitalise keeps coming down.

Challenges before Digital Economy

A well-functioning digital society requires that individuals acquire certain capabilities and skills so they can function effectively as digital citizens, consumers and employees. Education programmes need to provide citizens with digital literacy skills so they can use the internet to enhance their daily lives and navigate the online world with confidence in their ability to recognise and avoid abuses such as false data, fraud and offensive content.

A digital economy needs a digitally skilled workforce, which means employees who can use digital technology, handle large amounts of data and act with a high degree of flexibility and creativity. The advent of new technologies requires continuous upgrading of relevant skills as a prerequisite to remaining employable. Digital literacy and skills building not only need to be included in national curricula, they also must be made available to and used by working-age people and the elderly. Digital economies only grow if companies are online and taking advantage of technology to gain access to new customers and markets and to improve operations.

The ability of companies to make use of new technologies is potentially constrained by a shortfall in skilled labour—which means that demand for those skills and the willingness to pay for them, will rise. Already today, in many markets there is a big shortage of IT professionals and related functions. Ensuring timely and sufficient supply of these skill sets cannot be left to market forces alone.

Promoting Digital Payments within Government

Ministry of Electronics and Information Technology, Government of India envisages Paperless, Cashless and Faceless services across the country, especially in rural and remote parts of India. The Apex Committee on Digital India has recommended a targeted and time bound approach to implement digital payments for citizens across all the e-Services of Government Ministries and Departments. Against this backdrop, Ministry has notified Guideline for Electronic Payments and Receipts (EPR), intended for Central Public Sector Undertakings, State Governments, Govt. of India Autonomous Bodies, and Municipalities for expeditiously implementing appropriate mechanism to enable electronic payments and receipts.

The objective of this guideline is to provide guidelines for Departments to: (a) Assess various services involving payments and receipts by types of services and level of electronic payment enablement; (b) Provide actionable instructions for universal adoption of electronic payment modes for each type of service through various payment channels; and (c) Provide guidelines on engagement with various payment service providers (Source: official website of Cashless India).

Future Prospects of Cashless Payments in India

The rapid growth of smartphones, Internet penetration and e-commerce is complementing these; card payment volumes have been growing. Indian consumption is still dominated by cash, with cards contributing only 5 per cent of the personal consumption expenditure. In developed countries, 30-50 per cent of spends happen through cards. So there is huge growth opportunity. The credit card industry in India sees greater acceptance among consumers. According to Worldline India Card Payment Report 2014-15, the credit card base grew at 9.8 per cent in the past year. Worldline India is a leader in the payment and transactions services in the country. Alternative methods like mobile wallets and prepaid cash cards accounted for 3 per cent of digital transaction

The government needs to take the necessary steps and make some policy considerations when they are preparing for a cashless economy. The payment systems have to be protected from the cyber-attacks which are the major threat for cashless transactions. Also, the government should be able to serve the under banked as well. Everyone from the society should have access to an electronic system that they can use for such transactions (Tawade, 2017).

Chapter - 8

E-Marketing

E-Marketing is known as Internet Marketing, Web Marketing, Digital Marketing, or Online Marketing. E-marketing is the process of marketing a product or service using the Internet. E-marketing not only includes marketing on the Internet, but also includes marketing done via e-mail and wireless media. It uses a range of technologies to help connect businesses to their customers. It can be considered to be equivalent to Internet marketing and Digital Marketing. Most in the industry would look at it this way.

However, E-marketing is sometimes considered to have a broader scope than Internet marketing since it refers to digital media such as web, e-mail and wireless media, but also includes management of digital customer data and electronic customer relationship management systems (E-CRM systems).

Amazon

Amazon is an American electronic commerce and cloud computing company based in Seattle, Washington that was founded by Jeff Bezos on July 5, 1994. The tech giant is the largest Internet retailer in the world as measured by revenue and market capitalization, and second largest after Alibaba Group in terms of total sales. In 2015, Amazon surpassed Walmart as the most valuable retailer in the United States by market capitalization. Amazon is the fourth most valuable public company in the world, the largest Internet company by revenue in the world, and the eighth largest employer in the United States.

The company was founded as a result of what Jeff Bezos called his "regret minimization framework," which described his efforts to fend off any regrets for not participating sooner in the Internet business boom during that time. Bezos selected the name Amazon by looking through the dictionary; he settled on "Amazon" because it was a place that was "exotic and different", just as he had envisioned for his Internet enterprise. The Amazon River, he noted, was the biggest river in the world, and he planned to make his store the biggest bookstore in the world. In 2011, Amazon had 30,000 full-time employees in the USA, and by the end of 2016, it had 180,000 employees. The company employs 306,800 people worldwide in full and part-time jobs.

On October 18, 2011, Amazon.com announced a partnership with DC Comics for the exclusive digital rights to many popular comics, including Superman, Batman, Green Lantern, The Sandman, and Watchmen. In November 2013, Amazon.com announced a partnership with the United States Postal Service to begin delivering orders on Sundays. In July 2016, Amazon.com announced a partnership with the U.K. Civil Aviation Authority to test some of the technologies and may use delivery service via prime air drone in the future. In June 2017, Nike confirmed a partnership with Amazon, stating it to be in an initial phase where they'll be selling goods on Amazon. As of October 11, 2017, AmazonFresh sell a range of Booths branded products for home delivery in selected areas (Amazon, 2018).

eBay

eBay Inc. is a multinational e-commerce corporation based in San Jose, California that facilitates consumer-to-consumer and business-to-consumer sales through its website. It was founded by Pierre Omidyar in 1995, and became a notable success story of the dot-com bubble. The website is free to use for buyers, but sellers are charged fees for listing items after a limited number of free listings, and again when those items are sold. The company's business strategy includes increasing international trade. eBay is a publicly visible market which has attracted an interest from economists, who have used it to analyse aspects of buying and selling behaviour, auction formats, etc., comparing them with previous theoretical and empirical findings (source: Wikipedia).

Paytm

Paytm is an Indo-Chinese mobile-first financial services company that offers payments, banking, lending and insurance to consumers and merchants. It was founded by Vijay Shekhar Sharma in August 2010 and is based out of Delhi NCR, India. Paytm was founded in August 2010 with an initial investment of $2 million by its founder Vijay Shekhar Sharma. It started off as a Prepaid Mobile and DTH recharge platform and later it added Data Card, Postpaid Mobile and Landline Bill payments in 2013. In August 2015, the Reserve Bank of India granted 'in-principle' approval for Payments Bank to Paytm. In 2018, it set up Paytm Money to build Investment and Wealth Management offerings for its users. This business will bring direct mutual funds and money-market funds for the Indian masses.

In 2007, Paytm's parent One97 Communications Ltd. got its first institutional investor in Venture Capital firm SAIF Partners. In January 2018, Paytm Payments Bank partnered with IndusInd Bank to offer a super-liquid, linked Fixed Deposit with up to 6.85 per cent annual interest. In 2016, Paytm invested in logistics startups LogiNext and XpressBees (source: Wikipedia).

Flipkart

Flipkart is an Indian company serving in the electronic commerce sector and headquartered in Bengaluru, India. It was founded in October 2007 by Sachin Bansal and Binny Bansal. Flipkart was founded on 2007 by Sachin Bansal and Binny Bansal, both alumni of the Indian Institute of Technology Delhi. They worked for Amazon.com, and left to create their new company incorporated in October 2007 as Flipkart Online Services Pvt. Ltd.(source: Wikipedia).

Walmart

Walmart Inc. is an American multinational retail corporation that operates a chain of hypermarkets, discount department stores, and grocery stores. Headquartered in Bentonville, Arkansas, the company was founded by Sam Walton in 1962 and incorporated on October 31, 1969. It also owns and operates Sam's Club retail warehouses. As of January 31, 2018, Walmart has 11,718 stores and clubs in 28 countries, operating under 59 different names. The company debuted on the New York Stock Exchange in 1972.

Walmart is headquartered in the Walmart Home Office complex in Bentonville, Arkansas. The company's business model is based on selling a wide variety of general merchandise at low prices. Walmart's operations are organized into four divisions: Walmart U.S., Walmart International, Sam's Club and Global eCommerce. The company offers various retail formats throughout these divisions, including su per centers, supermarkets, hypermarkets, warehouse clubs, cash-and-carry stores, home improvement, specialty electronics, restaurants, apparel stores, drugstores, convenience stores, and digital retail. As of January 31, 2018, Walmart's international operations comprised 6,360 stores and 800,000 workers in 26 countries outside the United States. Walmart Argentina was founded in 1995 and, as of January 31, 2018, operates 106 stores(source: Wikipedia).

Myntra

Myntra is an Indian fashion e-commerce company headquartered in Bengaluru, Karnataka, India. The company was founded in 2007 to sell personalized gift items. By 2010, Myntra shifted to selling clothing. Established by Mukesh Bansal along with Ashutosh Lawania and Vineet Saxena, Myntra sold on-demand personalized gift items. In 2014 Myntra merged with Indian e-commerce company Flipkart.com in an estimated deal of 2,000 crores (US$310 million)(source: Wikipedia).

Snapdeal

Snapdeal is an Indian e-commerce company based in New Delhi, India. The company was started by Kunal Bahl and Rohit Bansal in February 2010. Snapdeal was started on 4 February 2010 as a daily deals platform, but expanded in September 2011 to become an online marketplace. Snapdeal has acquired several business enterprises. In June 2011, the online marketplace acquired Bengaluru-based group buying website, Grabbon.com.(source: Wikipedia).

Infibeam

Infibeam is an Indian internet and e-commerce conglomerate involved in online retailing, e-commerce software and internet services. The company is headquartered in Ahmedabad, India. It is an online retailer for books, electronics, and automobiles in India. Infibeam is listed on the National Stock Exchange of India. Infibeam was founded in 2007 by Vishal Mehta, a Cornell and MIT Sloan alumnus. After working for Dell and Amazon.com in the US for five years, Mehta returned to India in 2007 and started Infibeam along with a group of Amazon employees. Infibeam's businesses include online retailing through its flagship website 'infibeam.com', e-commerce platform software service through 'buildabazaar.com', e-commerce marketplace 'dhamaal.com' and its own branded e-book reader(source: Wikipedia).

Yepme

Yepme is an online shopping company headquartered in Gurgaon, Haryana, India. It was established in April 2011. The company specializes in the online retailing of men's and women's garments and accessories. Yepme.com, was launched in April 2011 by Vivek Gaur, Sandeep Sharma and Anand Jadhav. Gaur (CEO) has experience building successful online companies. The main target customer for Yepme.com is tier 2 and tier 3 towns, where the big apparel brands do not have many retail stores(source: Wikipedia).

Craftsvilla

Craftsvilla is an Indian e-commerce portal that sells ethnic apparel, footwear, fashion accessories, beauty products, handcrafted home accessories and other ethnic fashion and lifestyle products. The company is headquartered in Mumbai, Maharashtra. Craftsvilla.com uses an online marketplace model by aggregating artisans, designers and retailers from all over India onto a single platform and connects local artisans and designers directly to global customers. Craftsvilla has tied up with the Ministry of Textiles, Government of India, for e-marketing of handloom products from small weaver(source: Wikipedia).

ShopClues

Shop Clues is an online marketplace owned by Clues Network Pvt. Ltd. It was established in July 2011 in Silicon Valley by Sanjay Sethi, Sandeep Aggarwal and Radhika Aggarwal. It is based in Gurgaon, India. ShopClues focuses on unstructured categories of home and kitchen, fashion, electronics and daily utility items. In 2015, the e-commerce player launched its Android app for sellers, and later added Windows and iOS app.(source: Wikipedia).

HomeShop18

HomeShop18 is an Indian online and on-air shopping channel owned by the Network 18 Group division of Reliance Industries. The HomeShop18 television channel was launched on 9 April 2008. The television network can be currently seen on cable, satellite and some terrestrial channels in India. It also became the country's first ever 24/7 home shopping channel to be available on DD Free Dish reach, a free-to-air direct-to-home (DTH) broadcasting platform of Prasar Bharati. The channel has been made available from November 1, 2015(source: Wikipedia).

Jabong

Jabong.com is an Indian fashion and lifestyle e-commerce portal founded by Praveen Sinha, Lakshmi Potluri, Arun Chandra Mohan and Manu Jain. The portal sells apparel, footwear, fashion accessories, beauty products, fragrances, home accessories and other fashion and lifestyle products. It was co-founded by Arun Chandra Mohan, Praveen Sinha, Lakshmi Potluri and Manu Jain. All co-founders have left the company. Jabong.com launched the India Online Fashion Week in 2014. The event was described as a platform for young and aspiring designers, stylists, models and photographers who were mentored by fashion industry experts including celebrity mentor Yami Gautam(source: Wikipedia).

Chapter - 9

E-Commerce

E-Commerce is simply the sale and purchase of services and goods over and electronic medium, like the Internet. e-Commerce started way back in the 1960s when organisations began to use Electronic Data Interchange to transfer documents of their business back and forth. The 1990s saw the emergence of online shopping businesses, which is quite a phenomenon today. It is also known as e-Business, or electronic business. Ecommerce one of the highest growing business, with India having great market potential for investments. There has been huge surge in investment since last year and more is expected in coming years. The rapid growth in use of mobile and internet users has facilitated ecommerce business in both urban and rural cities.

What is E-Commerce?

Electronic commerce refers to a wide range of online business activities for products and services. It also pertains to "any form of business transaction in which the parties interact electronically rather than by physical exchanges or direct physical contact." E-commerce is usually associated with buying and selling over the Internet, or conducting any transaction involving the transfer of ownership or rights to use goods or services through a computer-mediated network.

E-commerce vs. E-business

While some use e-commerce and e-business interchangeably, they are distinct concepts. In e-commerce, information and communications technology is used in inter-business or inter-organizational transactions (transactions between and among firms/organizations) and in business-to-consumer transactions (transactions between firms/organizations and individuals).

In e-business, on the other hand, ICT is used to enhance one's business. It includes any process that a business organization (either a for-profit, governmental or non-profit entity) conducts over a computer-mediated network.

Types of E-Commerce

The major different kinds of e-commerce are: business-to-business (B2B); business-to-consumer (B2C); business-to-government (B2G); consumer-to-consumer (C2C); and mobile commerce (m-commerce). Let discuss the types:

- B2B e-commerce is simply defined as e-commerce between companies. This is the type of e-commerce that deals with relationships between and among businesses. About 80 per cent of e-commerce is of this type, and most experts predict that B2B e-commerce will continue to grow faster than the B2C segment.
- Business-to-consumer e-commerce, or commerce between companies and consumers, involves customers gathering information; purchasing physical goods (i.e., tangibles such as books or consumer products) or information goods (or goods of electronic material or digitized content, such as software, or e-books); and, for information goods, receiving products over an electronic network. The more common applications of this type of e-commerce are in the areas of purchasing products and information, and personal finance management, which pertains to the management of personal investments and finances with the use of online banking tools.
- Business-to-government e-commerce or B2G is generally defined as commerce between companies and the public sector. It refers to the use of the Internet for public procurement, licensing procedures, and other government-related operations. This kind of e-commerce has two features: first, the public sector assumes a pilot/leading role in establishing e-commerce; and second, it is assumed that the public sector has the greatest need for making its procurement system more effective.
- Consumer-to-consumer e-commerce or C2C is simply commerce between private individuals or consumers. This type of e-commerce is characterized by the growth of electronic marketplaces and

online auctions, particularly in vertical industries where firms/ businesses can bid for what they want from among multiple suppliers.16 It perhaps has the greatest potential for developing new markets.

- M-commerce (mobile commerce) is the buying and selling of goods and services through wireless technology-i.e., handheld devices such as cellular telephones and personal digital assistants (PDAs). Japan is seen as a global leader in m-commerce. (See https://en.wikibooks.org/wiki/E-Commerce_and_E-Business/ Concepts_and_Definitions)

Benefits of E-Commerce

Electronic Commerce is known as e-commerce that consists of the purchasing and selling of products or services through electronic systems like computer networks and the Internet. With increasing demand for online purchasing, more and more businesses are moving to e-store from brick and mortar stores. Today, e-Commerce has revolutionized the way companies are doing business. Now, consumers can purchase almost anything online 24*7 a day and get an ultimate shopping experience. Consumers can also get description and details from an online product catalog. For customers, it is very much important to get information about the product no matter whether the time of day and day of the week.

With e-commerce business, the suppliers can decrease the cost of managing their inventory of goods that they can automate the inventory management using web-based management system. Indirectly, they can save their operational costs. The best thing is e-commerce retailers can easily keep a constant eye on consumers' buying habits and interests to tailors their offer suit to consumers' requirements. For effective business transactions, e-commerce is an efficient and competence method. Setting-up cost is extremely low as compare to expanding your business with more brick and mortar locations. Very few licenses and permits are required to start-up an online business than physical store.

With lots of customers' reviews and product ratings, seller can easily increase sells as new customers find that products are good and effective. If selleris running a physical store, it will be limited by the geographical area that can service, but with an e-Commerce website, seller can sell products and services across the world. One of the most important benefits that ecommerce merchants can enjoy is store timings are now 24/7/365 as they can run e-commerce websites all the time.

As like e-commerce business can help B2B organizations to get new customers, so it will be helpful for e-commerce businesses to boost their brand awareness in the market. One of the most positive things about e-commerce is that seller can decrease the costs of business. One of the best benefits of ecommerce for customers is they can get huge information that is not possible in a physical store. With ecommerce platform, it becomes easy for businesses to launch channel specific and particular brand ecommerce website.

One of the most tangible positives of e-commerce is the lowered cost. A part of these lowered costs could be passed on to customers in the form of discounted prices. On an e-commerce website, customers can click through intuitive navigation or use a search box to narrow down their product search immediately. It is not unusual for customers to travel long distances to reach their preferred physical store. E-commerce allows them to visit the same store virtually, with just a few mouse clicks. E-commerce websites can make additional information easily available to customers. Most of this information is provided by vendors and does not cost anything to create or maintain.

E-commerce websites can run all the time. From the merchant's point of view, this increases the number of orders they receive. From the customer's point of view, an "always open" store is more convenient. According Markus (2017), "there are various benefits of e-commerce, like as

- Global market: A physical store will always be limited by a geographical area it can serve. An online store, or any other type of e-commerce business for that matter, has the whole world as its market. Going from a local customer base to a global market at no additional cost is really one of the greatest advantages of trading online.
- Around-the-clock availability: Another great benefit of running an online business is that it is always open. For a merchant, it's a dramatic increase in sales opportunities; for a customer, it's a convenient and immediately available option. Unrestricted by the working hours, e-commerce businesses can serve customers 24/7/365.
- Reduced costs:e-commerce businesses benefit from significantly lower running costs. As there's no need to hire sales staff or maintain a physical storefront, the major e-commerce costs go to

warehousing and product storage. And those running a drop shipping business enjoy even lower upfront investment requirements. As merchants are able to save on operational costs, they can offer better deals and discounts to their customers.

- Inventory management: e-commerce businesses can automate their inventory management by using electronic tools to accelerate ordering, delivery and payment procedures. It's saving businesses billions in operational and inventory costs.
- Targeted marketing: With access to such a wealth of customer data and an opportunity to keep an eye on customer buying habits as well as the emerging industry trends, e-commerce businesses can stay agile and shape their marketing efforts to provide a better-tailored experience and find more new customers. Just consider for a moment that you have a chance to address thousands of your customers by their first name; that is something already.
- Serving niche markets: Running a niche brick-and-mortar business is extremely difficult. There's almost no chance of scaling it unless a niche product becomes mainstream. By tapping into a global market, on the other hand, e-commerce retailers can build a highly profitable niche business without any further investment. Using online search capabilities, customers from any corner of the world can find and purchase your products.
- Working from anywhere: Often, running an e-commerce business means that you don't need to sit in an office from 9 to 5 or suffer through a commute day-in and day-out. A laptop and a good internet connection is all it takes to manage your business from anywhere in the world."

Disadvantages of E-Commerce

- Security and Integrity Issues: Hackers are adept at manipulating online business websites to harvest financial data. The information requires of customers — shipping address, credit card details and email — potentially provides a valuable resource for hackers to initiate identity theft. This risk keeps some people from shopping online. Seller have to assure customers of the security of their personal data as they interact with e-business. Ensure site integrity by investing time and money in learning and implementing good security measures, including digital signatures and data encryption, to protect client information lest it falls in the wrong hands and lawsuits ensue.

- Purchase to Delivery Time: As much as the Internet has the advantage of processing orders and payments in real time, this has little benefit to the customer who requires the purchased item equally fast. Unlike brick-and-mortar businesses, purchases from your e-business typically have a time lag from purchase to delivery of the physical goods. Some customers would rather go to the physical store and pick up the item unless it's of a digital kind, such as an e-book or music file.
- Momentary Intangibility: The personal touch is a missing factor in online transactions. An e-business normally offers the customer no physical proximity to the items purchased until delivery. Experiencing the feel, taste or smell of a product can influence the decision to buy.
- Sectoral Limitations: Not every company can participate in e-commerce. Some are challenged in terms of expertise and availability of technology, while others carry products that can't be shipped economically.

Steps for E-Payments

The most popular definition of E-Commerce is based on the online perspective of the conducted business. E-commerce provides the capability of buying and selling products, information and services on the Internet and other online environments. As for any trading activity, the issue of safe and reliable money exchange between transacting parties is essential. The merchant sells the goods to customer and customer pay the price with the help of E-Payment system.The following steps are carried out for payments during online procedures:

- The payment procedure is initiated by the applicant. The applicant selects a bank.
- A payment request is sent to the bank that contains an XML message with a redirection URL that points to the government application. In response, the bank opens a session and forwards the user to the given URL.
- The authority's application forwards the applicant on to the online banking application of his bank. After he has been authenticated, the payment transaction is carried out.
- Before the transaction is carried out, the bank checks if there is still a connection open between the bank and the authority.

- After the connection is confirmed by the authority, the bank carries out the money transfer.
- A confirmation message is sent to the authority stating whether the payment was successful or not.
- The authority responds with an acknowledgement message.
- The payment process is finalized and the applicant is referred back to the authorities application.

Types of E-payment System

According the article of Kaur & Pathak (2015), types of e-payment system are as below:

- **Credit cards:** A Credit card is a piece of plastic, 3-1/8inches by 2-1/8 inches in size, that carries information that allow you to make purchase now pay for them later. Credit cards from visa maser card or any other network allow you to pay for purchase or services by borrowing from the credit card company. To purchase goods from merchant who accept credit card such as merchant has credit card reader to purchase the payment transaction to withdraw cash from ATM.
- **Debit Card:** Debit card is a prepaid card and also known as ATM card. An individual has to open an account with the issuing bank which gives debit card with a personal id number, when he makes a purchase he enters his pin number on shop pin pad. When the card is slurped through the electronic terminal it dials the acquire a banking system either master card or visa card that validate the pin and finds out from the issuing bank whether to accept or decline the transaction the customer can never overspend because the system reject any transaction which exceeds the balance in his account the bank never face a default because the amount spent is debited immediately from the customer account.
- **Smart card:** Smart card was first introduce in Europe most of these method is known as stored value card. A smart card is about the size of a credit card, made of a plastic with an embedded microprocessor chip that holds important financial and personal information. The microprocessor chip is loaded with the relevant information and periodically recharged. In addition to these pieces of information, systems have been developed to store cash onto the chip. The money on the card is saved in an encrypted form and is protected by a password to ensure the security of the smart card solution.

- **Digital Wallet:** Electronic wallets being very useful for frequent online shoppers are commercially available for pocket, palm-sized, handheld, and desktop PCs. They offer a secure, convenient, and portable tool for online shopping. They store personal and financial information such as credit cards, passwords, PINs, and much more. To facilitate the credit-card order process, many companies are introducing electronic wallet services. E-wallets allow you to keep track of your billing and shipping information so that it can be entered with one click at participating merchants' sites.
- **Electronic Cheque:** Electronic cheque is messages that contain all the information that is found on an ordinary Cheque but it uses digital signature for signing and endorsing and has digital certificate to authenticate bank account. There are many websites that accept Electronic Cheque. An electronic payment process that resembles the function of paper cheques butoffers great security and more feature. Electronic checks are typically used in orders processed online and are governed by the same laws that apply to paper checks.
- **Electronic cash:**Similar to regular cash, e-cash enables transactions between customers without the need for banks or other third parties. When used, e-cash is transferred directly and immediately to the participating merchants and vending machines. Electronic cashes a secure and convenient alternative to bills and coins. E-cash usually operates on a smartcard, which includes an embedded microprocessor chip. The microprocessor chip stores cash value and the security features that make electronic transactions secure. when e cash created by one bank is accepted by other reconciliation must occur without any problem cash must be storable and receivable (Kaur & Pathak, 2015).

Table 8.1: Comparisons of E-Payment System

Feature	*Credit Card*	*E-Cash*	*E-Cheque*	*Smart card*	*Debit Card*
Actual payment time	Paid later	Prepaid	Prepaid	Prepaid	Prepaid
Online and offline transactions	Online transactions	Online transactions	Offline transfers	Offline transfers	Offline transfers
Bank account involvement	Credit card account makes the payment.	No involvement	account makes the payment.	account makes the payment	account makes the payment

(*Contd...*)

Users	Any legitimate credit card users.	Anyone	Anyone with a bank account.	Anyone with a bank or credit card account.	Anyone with a bank or credit card account.
Party to which payment is made out	Distributing bank	Store	Store	Store	Store
Small payments	Transaction costs are high. Not suitable for small payments.	Transaction costs are low, suitable for small payments.	Allows stores to accumulate debts until it reaches a limit before paying for it. Suitable for small payments.	Transaction costs are low. Allows stores to accumulate debts until it reaches a limit before paying for it. Therefore, it is suitable for small payments.	Transaction costs are low. Allows stores to accumulate debts until it reaches a limit before paying for it. Therefore, it is suitable for small payments.
Transaction information face value	Can be signed and issued freely in compliance with the limit.	Face value is often set, and cannot be changed.	Can be signed and issued freely in compliance with the limit.	Can be deducted freely in compliance with the limit.	Can be deducted freely in compliance with the limit.
Limit on transfer.	Depends on the limit of the credit card.	Depends on how much is prepaid	No limit	Depends on how much money is saved.	Depends on how much money is saved
Mobility	Yes.	No.	No.	Yes.	Yes.

Source: Kaur, K. & Pathak, A. (2015). E-Payment System on E-Commerce in India, International Journal of Engineering Research and Applications, Vol. 5, Issue 2, (Part -1), pp. 81-82.

Component of Effective Electronic Payment System

- Consumer and browser: A consumer interact with the online commerce system through a web browser typically a consumer first accessing a shopping mall and then uses the hyperlink from the mall to access the merchant home page.
- Shopping mall: A shopping mall is where most consumer first visit for a shipping free there will be several shopping malls and it may pay to enlist with one or more well-known mall.
- Merchant systems: It consists of the home page and related software to manage the business.
- Banking network: it consists of several components there is bank that processes the online financial transaction for the given merchant the bank maintains the account for the merchant authorize and processes the payment the merchant bank also maintains a link with the consumer bank for verifying the trans actions (Kaur & Pathak, 2015).

Digital Payment Requirement

For any digital payment system to succeed.
The criteria given in table ought to be satisfied.

Criteria	*Need for the criteria*
Acceptability	Payment infrastructure need to be widely accepted.
Anonymity	Identify of the customer should be protected.
Convertibility	Digital money should be convertibility it any type of fund.
Efficiency	Cost per transaction should be near to zero.
Integration	Integration should be crated support existing system.
Security	Should flow financial transaction over open network.
Reliability	Should avoid single point of failure.
Usability	Payment should be easy as in the real word.
Scalability	Infrastructure should not break down if new customer and merchant join.

Source: Kaur, K. & Pathak, A. (2015). E-Payment System on E-Commerce in India, International Journal of Engineering Research and Applications, Vol. 5, Issue 2, (Part -1), p. 81.

E-Commerce in India

India has an internet users base of about 450 million as of July 2017, 40 per cent of the population. Despite being the second-largest user base in world, only behind China (650 million, 48 per cent of population), the penetration of e-commerce is low compared to markets. In 2015, the largest e-commerce companies in India were Flipkart, Snapdeal, Amazon India, and Paytm. India's e-commerce market was worth about $3.9 billion in 2009, it went up to $12.6 billion in 2013. In 2013, the e-retail segment was worth US$2.3 billion. About 70 per cent of India's e-commerce market is travel related. According to Google India, there were 35 million online shoppers in India in 2014 Q1 and was expected to cross 100 million mark by end of year 2016.

According to a study conducted by the Internet and Mobile Association of India, the e-commerce sector is estimated to reach Rs 211,005 crores by December 2016. The study also stated that online travel accounts for 61 per cent of the e-commerce market. As per "India Goes Digital", a report by Avendus Capital, the Indian e-commerce market is estimated at Rs 28,500 Crore ($6.3 billion) for the year 2011. Online travel constitutes a sizable portion (87 per cent) of this market today. India has got its own version of Cyber Monday known as Great Online Shopping Festival which started in December 2012, when Google India partnered with e-commerce companies including Flipkart, HomeShop18, Snapdeal, Indiatimes shopping and Makemytrip.

The e-commerce has transformed the way business is done in India. The Indian e-commerce market is expected to grow to US$ 200 billion by 2026 from US$ 38.5 billion as of 2017. The value of e-commerce market is expected to cross US$ 50 billion by 2018. The Indian consumer internet market is expected to grow by 44 per cent year-on-year to touch US$ 65 billion in 2017, up from US$ 45 billion in 2016. The internet industry in India is likely to double to reach US$ 250 billion by 2020, growing to 7.5 per cent of Gross Domestic Product (GDP), with the number of mobile internet users growing to about 650 million and that of high-speed internet users reaching 550 million.

Since 2014, the Government of India has announced various initiatives namely, Digital India, Make in India, Start-up India, Skill India and Innovation Fund. The timely and effective implementation of such programs will likely support the e-commerce growth in the country. The e-commerce industry been directly impacting the micro, small & medium enterprises in India by providing means of financing, technology and training and has a favourable cascading effect on other industries as well.

Amazon is already deeply committed to the country, where it has pledged to deploy more than $5 billion to grow its business, and now U.S. rival Walmart is said to be inching closer to a deal to buy Flipkart. Bloomberg reports that Walmart is poised to acquire 60-80 per cent of the company for $12 billion. The deal could potentially value Flipkart as high a $20 billion, which would be a major jump on the $12 billion valuation it secured in 2016 when it landed a $1.4 billion investment from Microsoft, Tencent and eBay. Walmart's increased focus on India comes after the retailer exited the Chinese market in 2016, selling its Yihaodian service to Alibaba rival JD.com. Amazon itself is keen to diversify. The company recently announced it has more than 100 million Prime members worldwide, having added "more members in India in its first year. Outside of Flipkart and Amazon, Alibaba has invested considerably in Paytm, which specializes in mobile payments but also includes e-commerce, digital banking and has plans for gaming (Russell, 2018).

Cyber Crime

Cybercrimes can be defined as: "Offences that are committed against individuals or groups of individuals with a criminal motive to intentionally harm the reputation of the victim or cause physical or mental harm, or loss, to the victim directly or indirectly, using modern telecommunication networks such as Internet (networks including but not limited to Chat rooms, emails, notice boards and groups) and mobile phones (Bluetooth/SMS/MMS)". Cybercrimes crossing international borders and involving the actions of at least one nation state is sometimes referred to as cyberwarfare.

Cybercrimes are crimes which are: (a) directed at computers or other devices (for example, hacking), and (b) where computers or other devices are integral to the offence (for example, online fraud, identity theft and the distribution of child exploitation material). Common types of cybercrime include hacking, online scams and fraud, identity theft, attacks on computer systems and illegal or prohibited online content.

According the article of Gupta (2018), Cyber-crime in India is categorised into four types which include:

1. **Cyber-crime against person:** This type of cyber-crime is committed against a person using an electronic domain as a medium. Cyber-crime against a person includes:

- Cyber stalking: Cyber stalking is online harassment, when a person is stalked using internet as a medium. Generally, the stalker is aware of his victim and instead of stalking them in reality, the stalker keeps a track of a person's online activities to stalk his victim. A Stalker can use the internet, emails, SMS, webcams, phones calls, websites or even videos to harass his target.
- Hacking: Hacking means getting an unauthorised access to someone's personal information for illegal gains or misuse. Hackers get access to the user's personal and sensitive information. They can also monitor every online activity of a person like logging in, credentials added, banking transactions made, etc.
- Cracking: Cracking refers to digitally removing the Copyright protection code which prevents copied or pirated software from working on computers which do not have the Software vendor or owner's authorisation. The person who is involved in such activity is different from a hacker and is known as a cracker. Cracker uses his knowledge to break the cyber law and tampers with the computer.
- Defamation: Online or cyber defamation involves damaging someone's reputation using a computer or the internet as a medium. This is done by writing a derogatory statement about a person on social media, posting vulgar pictures or videos, etc.
- Online Fraud: Online fraud is one of the most common types of cyber-crime. It involves stealing a person's sensitive information like banking credentials by using phishing sites and withdrawing money from victim's account. Online lottery scams are also rampant these days; one such example is the Nigeria lottery scams.

- Dissemination of Obscene Material: It includes distribution of obscene materials or pornography on social media. It includes hosting of websites containing pornographic material which has a tendency to deprave or corrupt the minds of individuals.
- Child pornography: Circulation of any material that has a tendency to deprave the mind of the minor children is also a cyber-crime. It involves the use of electronic devices to create, distribute or access material which is obscene in nature and have a tendency to corrupt young minds.
- Spoofing: Spoofing involves misrepresentation of the origin of any data. While an Email/SMS is generated from one source, it shows that it has been generated from another. Cyber criminals use this means to get personal information of the user like bank details, etc.
- Phishing: It involves sending spam emails to the user while claiming to be an established enterprise in order to obtain his personal information and steal the user's identity.

2. **Cyber Crime against property:** Cyber-crime against property is committed using an electronic device as a medium. Here, the property does not mean any immovable property but includes movable and intangible property like computers, Intellectual Property, etc. Different cyber-crimes against property are:

- Transmitting virus: A computer virus is a malware programme that infects the files, disk drives, and computer programmes. Programmes that multiply like viruses and spread from computer to computer are called 'worms'. Virus, Worms, Trojan Horse, Time bomb, Logic Bomb, Rabbit, and Bacterium are some examples of malicious software that infect the computer.
- Cybersquatting: Cybersquatting is when two or more persons claim the same domain name. Squatting is unlawfully occupying an uninhabited place. The hacker claims that he was the first one to use the domain name before the actual owner of the domain name.
- Cyber Vandalism: It involves the destruction of data on any electronic medium during the period when the network service is not available.
- Intellectual Property Crimes: IPRs are intangible property rights. IPR thefts are the most common cyber-crime in India and include

online piracy, software piracy, infringement of patents, designs, trademark, copyright, theft of source code, etc.

3. **Cyber-crime against Government:** The government of a country may become the target of a cyber-crime. A cyber-crime against a government is committed to threaten the unity, honour and security of the target country. Cyber-crime against government includes:

- Cyber Warfare: Cyber warfare is an Internet-based war conflict wherein the cyber-crime is politically motivated. It can disable official websites and networks, disrupt essential services such as Internet connection, steal classified data such as Sensex details and break down sensitive data like the payment gateway.
- Cyber Terrorism: It is an act of creating fear in the mind of people by using the internet as a medium. Section 66-F of the Information Technology Act, 2002 deals with cyber terrorism in India.

4. **Cyber-crime against society:** When a cyber-crime is committed against numerous individuals, it is known as cyber-crime against society. Cyber-crime against society include:

- Online Gambling: Gambling is prohibited in India under the Public Gambling Act, 1867. Online gambling is illegal all over India, except in Sikkim.
- Cyber Trafficking: Trafficking involves dealing in illegal trade activities such as trafficking women, slaves or children using the internet as a medium. (Source: https://www.myadvo.in/blog/cyber-crime-in-india/).

Cybercrime cases in India, registered under the IT Act, increased at a rate of 300 per cent between 2011 and 2014. In 2015, there were 11,592 cases of cybercrime registered in India. The Information Technology Act, 2000 passed by the Parliament of India in May 2000, had aimed to curb cybercrimes and to provide a legal framework for e-commerce transactions.

Information Technology Act, 2000

The Information Technology Act, 2000 (also known as ITA-2000, or the IT Act) is an Act of the Indian Parliament (No 21 of 2000) notified on 17 October 2000. It is the primary law in India dealing with cybercrime and electronic commerce. The Act provides legal framework for electronic governance by giving recognition to electronic records and digital signatures. The formations of Controller of Certifying Authorities was directed by the Act, to regulate issuing of digital signatures. It also defines cyber-crimes and prescribed penalties for them. It also established a Cyber Appellate Tribunal to resolve disputes rising from this new law. The Act also amended various sections of Indian Penal Code, 1860, Indian Evidence Act, 1872, Banker's Book Evidence Act, 1891, and Reserve Bank of India Act, 1934 to make them compliant with new technologies.

A major amendment was made in 2008. It introduced the Section 66A which penalized sending of "offensive messages". It also introduced the Section 69, which gave authorities the power of "interception or monitoring or decryption of any information through any computer resource". It also introduced for child porn, cyber terrorism and voyeurism. It was passed on 22 December 2008 without any debate in Lok Sabha. The next day it was passed by the Rajya Sabha. It was signed by the then President (Pratibha Patil) on 5 February 2009. On 13 April 2015, it announced that the Ministry of Home Affairs would form a committee of officials from the Intelligence Bureau, Central Bureau of Investigation, National Investigation Agency, Delhi Police and ministry itself to produce a new legal framework.

Chapter - 10

E-Banking

Online banking is an electronic payment system that enables customers of a bank or other financial institution to conduct a range of financial transactions through the financial institution's website.To access a financial institution's online banking facility, a customer with internet access will need to register with the institution for the service, and set up a password and other credentials for customer verification. It is also known as internet banking. In this 21st century, internet has been comprehensive used by many estate of person such as businessman use it to expansion their business to advertise their products and services. In addition, students use it to consort together with their friends either in nation or oversea and mostly already replace from mobile phone. Mostly people use internet to find the information what they want to know and internet will help them to search and settle the problem they face.

Digital Banking may be viewed as adoption of various existing and emerging technologies by the banks, in concert with associated changes in internal operations as well as external relationships for providing superior customer services and experiences effectively and efficiently. Technology is enabling banks to provide the convenience of anytime-anywhere-banking. Banks are now reengineering the way in which their services can be reached to their customers by bringing in flexibility in their "distribution channels".

To save more time, digital banking become a new age of banking program. Online banking payment is defined that through internet to transfer funds or money from one account to another account to develop banking activity such as paying loans or bills, shifting funds, inspecting account details and balances. Besides that, users also can pay mortgages and buying futures, warrants, options and others through online banking payments. So that, online banking payments can also be intituled internet banking payment.

Internet Banking

Internet banking refers to the use of Internet as a remote delivery channel for banking services such as opening a deposit account or transferring funds at different accounts etc. Further, it is a desirable opportunity for banks where the key to success is customer adoptionThe basic characteristics of internet banking are:

- To help bank perspective to save costs.
- To save time and money.
- To minimize the likelihood committing errors.
- To fulfil undergraduate student's convenience.
- To lower the transaction costs.

The features available through online banking:

- View balances: Checking balance doesn't require much work. Simply select account balances and take a look at balance and past transactions. If have more than one account, can also do transfers between accounts.
- Pay bills: To pay bills online, just need to add account the names of the companies wish to pay bills to. In the Pay Bills section, select Add payees, search for the name of the company and fill in the account number for each company.
- Transfer funds: When select Transfer Funds, be asked where to transfer the money to and from, when, and the amount.
- Set up recurring bill payments or transfers: If make a regular payment every month, it might be convenient to set up an automatic withdrawal from account.
- Monitor CIBC investments: If have any CIBC investments, can keep an eye on those stocks or mutual funds here.
- Send and receive an INTERAC e-TransferTM2: The recipient will get an e-mail notifying them of the transaction.
- View CIBC VISA accounts: Always a good place to monitor spending. Person can make credit card payments online, right from account.

Factor Influence Internet Banking

According to ukessays.com, factor influence internet banking are:

- **Security:** security concern is main barrier for internet banking is concluding by the banks. Main reason for slow growth of internet banking were discover by the security concern.New innovation of the level of the security or risk associated will influence the acceptance and adoption. Where internet banking has been long set up, the main significant factors that will slow down the progress of this new innovation is the main concern for security over the financial transaction via internet.Lack of security and reliability of transaction via internet is the main reason for they agree to refuse to use the internet banking. Security and privacy issues are concern by individual because they are still reluctant to use.Poor security is inadequate to protect customer's personal data.
- **Trust:** Trust is defined as a willingness to be susceptible to the action of the others. Define trust as a necessary component in a relationship especially whenever risk and uncertainty exist.Context of internet banking, trust has been suggested to be the one of the barrier that will hinder individuals from adopt the technology.Trust in the internet increase long term internet usage in the adoption decision. Trust will give guarantee safety for using internet banking.One of the important reasons is lack of trust make people do not use internet banking, so must improve application security and privacy only can give undergraduate student confidence for using internet banking.Trust is an antecedent of perceived usefulness, also perceived ease of use is an antecedent of trust. Trust has a directly and indirectly effect on behaviour intention to use.
- **Privacy protection:** Defined privacy as the protection of personal information so it is not reveal to or used by others.Privacy has been an important factor in the choice not to use internet banking. Effective privacy protection laws will consider the internet environment will help to build trust and confidence.To improve privacy issues, first banks must provide consumer reassurance and information, ensure consumer information would not disclose to other or third parties. Banks need to improve the application security and privacy and ensure bank information security and privacy. To assist consumer in development secure internet banking practice and risk management procedures.

- **Attitude:** Define attitude as person positive and negative feeling about internet banking adoption. Age will affect the attitude of individual toward internet banking. Attitude toward adoption and use of internet banking might give undergraduate student a positively image assuming security of internet transaction is safety enough.Personal banking experiences will affect attitude toward internet banking. Internet to user's banking needs to relate to the advantage the mount up to the user of the technology. show that relative advantage is very important factor to influence adoption of new innovation. Commonly, perceived relative advantage is positively connected to the rate of adoption.
- **Perceived ease of use:** Defined perceived ease of use as degree to which person believes that adopt internet banking would be free of effort.It is essential for the internet to be ease of use to increase the adoption rate of internet banking.
- **Awareness:** Explanation of Awareness can be the acceptance and continued to use the service, product or idea. Lack of awareness is the most common and important factor that negatively influence adoption of internet banking stated by. Try to inform the undergraduate student about the features, advantage and the benefit of internet banking, people normally are more prefer everything's conveniences. Lack of internet awareness is due to the internet banking services are still unaccepted.
- **Cost and Accessibility:** Cost as a characteristics of internet banking. Price or cost is one of the important factors that will affect the undergraduate adoption of innovation. Two types of costs are involved in the internet banking, first is bank charge and cost, second is the normal cost that associated with the internet activities. Banks must lower the transaction cost, to save costs. internet banking is very beneficial because of the savings in cots, time and space it offers; and also it is quick feedback to all the complaints. Saving transaction cost can improve customer service, increasing market reach and reducing costs are now basic expectation of internet banking services. Accessibility to computer or internet will affect the decision to adopt internet banking. (Source: https://www.ukessays.com/essays/project-management/the-characteristics-of-internet-banking.php)

Mobile Banking

Mobile banking is a service provided by a bank or other financial institution that allows its customers to conduct financial transactions remotely using a mobile device such as a smartphone or tablet. Unlike the related internet banking it uses software, usually called an app, provided by the financial institution for the purpose. Mobile banking is usually available on a 24-hour basis.

SMS Banking

SMS banking is a form of mobile banking. It is a facility used by some banks or other financial institutions to send messages (also called notifications or alerts) to customers' mobile phones using SMS messaging, or a service provided by them which enables customers to perform some financial transactions using SMS.Such banking services may use either push and pull messages. Push messages are those that a bank sends out to a customer's mobile phone, without the customer initiating a request for the information. Pull messages are initiated by the customer, using a mobile phone, for obtaining information or performing a transaction in the bank account.

Benefits of E-Banking

According the website of UKESSAYS, benefits of e-banking are:

For Banks

- Price: In the long run a bank can save on money by not paying for tellers or for managing branches. Plus, it's cheaper to make transactions over the Internet.
- Customer Base: The Internet allows banks to reach a whole new market- and a well off one too, because there are no geographic boundaries with the Internet. The Internet also provides a level playing field for small banks who want to add to their customer base.
- Efficiency: Banks can become more efficient than they already are by providing Internet access for their customers. The Internet provides the bank with an almost paper less system.
- Customer Service and Satisfaction: Banking on the Internet not only allow the customer to have a full range of services available to them but it also allows them some services not offered at any of the branches. The person does not have to go to a branch where that service may or may not be offer. A person can print of information, forms, and applications via the Internet and be able

to search for information efficiently instead of waiting in line and asking a teller. With better and faster options, a bank will surely be able to create better customer relations and satisfaction.

- Image: A bank seems more state of the art to a customer if they offer Internet access. A person may not want to use Internet banking but having the service available gives a person the feeling that their bank is on the cutting image.

For Customers

- Bill Pay: Bill Pay is a service offered through Internet banking that allows the customer to set up bill payments to just about anyone. Customer can select the person or company whom he wants to make a payment and Bill Pay will withdraw the money from his account and send the payee a paper check or an electronic payment.
- Other Important Facilities: E- banking gives customer the control over nearly every aspect of managing his bank accounts. Besides the Customers can, Buy and Sell Securities, Check Stock Market Information, Check Currency Rates, Check Balances, see which checks are cleared, Transfer Money, View Transaction History and avoid going to an actual bank. The best benefit is that Internet banking is free. At many banks the customer doesn't have to maintain a required minimum balance. The second big benefit is better interest rates for the customer.

National Electronic Funds Transfer

National Electronic Funds Transfer is a nation-wide payment system. Under this Scheme, individuals can electronically transfer funds from any bank branch to any individual having an account with any other bank branch in the country participating in the Scheme. Such transactions are settled in batches. Any transaction initiated after a designated settlement batch would have to wait till the next designated settlement batch.

Real-Time Gross Settlement

Real-time gross settlement systems are specialist funds transfer systems where the transfer of money or securities takes place from one bank to another on a "real time" and on a "gross" basis. Settlement in "real time" means a payment transaction is not subjected to any waiting period, with transactions being settled as soon as they are processed. "Gross settlement" means the transaction is settled on one-to-one basis without bundling or netting with any other transaction. "Settlement" means that once processed, payments are final and irrevocable. RTGS systems are usually operated by a country's central bank as it is seen as a critical infrastructure for a country's economy.

Immediate Payment Service

Immediate Payment Service is an instant real-time inter-bank electronic funds transfer system in India. It offers an inter-bank electronic fund transfer service through mobile phones. Unlike NEFT and RTGS, the service is available 24/7 throughout the year including bank holiday

E-Banking Revolution in India

In India, Reserve Bank of India outlined the mission to ensure that payment and settlement systems are safe, efficient, interoperable, authorized, accessible, inclusive and compliant with international standards. The Vision is to proactively encourage electronic payment system for ushering in a less cash society in India.Electronic Clearing Service was launched in 1990s to cater to bulk and repetitive payments. By September 2008, a new avatar in the form of National Electronic Clearing cell was launched to handle multiple credits to beneficiary accounts. National Electronic Clearing Service (NECS) rides on core banking solution of member banks (Dhananjay&Chandra, 2015).

Digital India, a much ambitious programme, was launched on 1st of July (Wednesday) in 2015 at the Indira Gandhi Indoor Stadium, Delhi. It was launched in the presence of various top industrialists (Tata Group chairman Cyrus Mistry, RIL Chairman and Managing Director Mukesh Ambani, Wipro Chairman Azim Premji, etc). In the meeting, they shared their ideas of bringing digital revolution to mass people of India from cities to villages. Various events have been held in the presence of Information Technology companies to cover 600 districts in the country. Digital India programme is a big step taken by the government of India to make this country a digitally empowered country. Various schemes regarding this plan have been unveiled (worth more than Rs 1 lakh crore) such as Digital Locker, e-health, e-education, national scholarship portal, e-sign, etc.

Digital India consists of three core components. They are (1)Development of secure and stable Digital Infrastructure, (2)Delivering government services digitally, and (3) Universal Digital Literacy. Digital India has the mission of making India digitally empowered and literate and all the services will be given online which made people to get information easily and in all languages, it wants all the services be available to its citizens digitally which will make our country empowered and more developed economy.

The new innovative digital technologies and futuristic thought processes have given birth to whole new businesses and social dimensions. Projects such as Make in India and Digital India are now the buzzwords to a bright and sustainable industrial and financial progress of our nation. As part of its impetus for Digital transformation in India, Government also encourages technology adoption / upgradation while providing connectivity with high speed bandwidth to every nook and corner of the country. The need for computerization was felt in the Indian banking sector in late 1980s, in order to improve the customer service, book-keeping and MIS reporting. In 1988, Reserve Bank of India set up a Committee on computerization in banks headed by Dr. C. Rangarajan. The process of Computerization gained pace with the opening of the economy in 1991-92. A major driver for this change was propelled by rising competition from private and foreign banks. Several commercial banks started moving towards digital customer services to remain competitive and relevant in the race.

Advantages of E-banking

There are some advantages to using e-banking both for banks and customers:

- Permanent access to the bank
- Access anywhere using mobile or computer
- Less time consuming
- Very safe and secure method
- Helps to transfer the money immediately and accurately
- Easy to use

Automated Teller Machine

An automated teller machine or automatic teller machine is an electronic computerized telecommunications device that allows a financial institution's customers to directly use a secure method of communication to access their bank accounts, order or make cash withdrawals and check their account balances without the need for a human bank teller.

National Payments Corporation of India

National Payments Corporation of India is the umbrella organisation for all retail payment systems in India, which aims to allow all Indian citizens to have unrestricted access to e-payment services. Founded in 2008, it is a not-for-profit organisation registered under section 8 of the Companies Act 2013. It has successfully completed the development of a domestic card payment network called RuPay, reducing the dependency on international card schemes.

National Financial Switch

National Financial Switch is the largest network of shared automated teller machines in India. It was designed, developed and deployed by the Institute for Development and Research in Banking Technology in 2004, with the goal of inter-connecting the ATMs in the country and facilitating convenience banking. It is run by the National Payments Corporation of India. The National Financial Switch was launched by the IDRBT on 27 August 2004, connecting the ATMs of three banks, Corporation Bank, Bank of Baroda and ICICI Bank. It is the largest domestic ATM network in the country member banks has been in the fore front in providing inter bank ATM services to maximum customers.

National Automated Clearing House

National Automated Clearing House introduced by National Payments Corporation of India, is a centralised clearing service that aims at providing interbank high volume, low value transactions that are repetitive and periodic in nature. According to the service's website, "NACH System can be used for making bulk transactions towards distribution of subsidies, dividends, interest, salary, pension etc. and also for bulk transactions towards collection of payments pertaining to telephone, electricity, water, loans, investments in mutual funds, insurance premium etc."

Core Banking Solution

Core banking is normally defined as the business conducted by a banking institution with its retail and small business customers. Many banks treat the retail customers as their core banking customers and have a separate line of business to manage small business.

Core Banking Solution is networking of bank branches, which allows customers to manage their accounts, and use various banking facilities from any part of the world. Execution of Core banking system across all branches helps to speed up most of the common transactions of bank and customer. In Core banking, the all branches access banking applications from centralized server which is hosted in secured datacentre. Banking software/ application performs basic operations like maintaining transactions, balance of withdrawal & payment, interest calculations on deposits & loans etc. This banking applications are deployed on centralized server & can be accessed using internet from any location.

Features of Core Banking are

- Customer relationship management features including a 360-degree customer view.
- The ability to originate new products and customers.
- Banking analytics including risk analysis, profitability analysis and provisions for capital reserve allocation and collateral management.
- Banking finance including general ledger and reporting.
- Banking channels such as teller systems, side counter applications, mobile banking and online banking solutions.
- Governance and compliance capabilities such as internal controls management and auditing.
- Core banking solutions to help maximize growth, increase productivity and mitigate risk.

Benefits of Core Banking

Core Banking Solutions enable the banks to provide exceptional customer services. It not only allows customers to access bank accounts from any interconnected branch across the world – it also gives the customers a chance to manage their bank accounts any time during the day from anywhere in the world. It helps the frontline staff manage the customer database easily, streamline general ledger and reporting and reduces the work load by completely or partially automating certain tasks such as telebanking.

Core Banking Solutions enable banks to handle the volume of customers more efficiently. Online banking reduces the number of footfalls in the bank branches every day. This enables the bank to cut down infrastructural, operational and support expenses to a great deal. ATM, Internet Banking. The modern Core Banking Solutions are designed to consolidate several stand-alone applications and optimize the costs associated with the maintenance of legacy systems. It allows banks to cut down on IT maintenance costs by moving to a shared services platform, which in turn also results in improvement of bank-end efficiency of the branches.

Most of the modern Core Banking Solutions come integrated with applications for business analytics. This helps in accessing the valuable information in the data collected in the back-end systems and turn it into actionable insights on a need basis. Several Core Banking Solutions provide customized as well real time data on any dimension.

Table 10.1: Basic Difference Between NEFT, RTGS and IMPS

	NEFT	*RTGS*	*IMPS*
Minimum transfer value	Rs.1	Rs.2 lakh	Rs.1
Maximum transfer value	No limit	Rs.10 lakh	Rs.2 lakh
Type of settlement	Batches	One-on-one settlement	One-on-one settlement
Speed of settlement	2 hours (subject to cut-off timings and batches)	Immediately	Immediately
Service availability	Weekdays: 12 batches between 8:00 a.m. - 6:30 p.m. Saturday: 6 batches between 8:00 a.m. 1:00 p.m. Sunday and bank holidays: Unavailable	Weekdays: 8:00 a.m. - 4:00 p.m Saturdays: 9:00 a.m. - 4:30 p.m Sunday and bank holidays: Unavailable	24/7
Transaction fee	Up to Rs.10,000 - Rs.2.50 From Rs.10,000 up to Rs.1 lakh - Rs.5 From Rs.1 lakh up to Rs.2 lakh - Rs.15 From Rs.2 lakh up to Rs.5 lakh - Rs.25 From Rs.5 lakh up to Rs.10 lakh - Rs.50	Between Rs.2 lakh up to Rs.5 lakh - Rs.25 From Rs.5 lakh up to Rs.10 lakh - Rs.50	Up to Rs.10,000 - Rs.2.5 From Rs.10,000 up to Rs.1,00,000 - Rs.5 From Rs.1,00,000 up to Rs.2,00,000 - Rs.15
Online/Offline	Both	Both	Online

Source: https://www.bankbazaar.com/ifsc/difference-neft-rtgs-imps.html

Bibliography

Articles/Reports

- Bhattacharyya, R. & Mehta, S. (2016). Demonetisation –Worst Effected the Small Traders, International Journal of Latest Technology in Engineering, Management & Applied Science, Volume V, Issue XII, pp.52-57.
- CHOE SANG-HUN (2009), North Korea Revalues Its Currency, Retrieved frm https://www.nytimes.com/2009/12/02/business/global/02korea.html
- Dash, A. (2017). A study on socio economic effect of demonetization in India, International Journal of Management and Applied Science, Volume-3, Issue-3, pp. 13-15.
- Dash, S. & Bagha, P. (2017). Impact of Demonetization on Stock Price Movements in Banking Sector of India, International Journal of Research and Scientific Innovation, Volume IV, Issue VIIS, pp.33-36.
- Dcosta, L., Raksha, R., Sasidharan, S., Varun, T., Rathnakumar, R., and Jagannathan, U. (2017), Analysis of Impact of Demonetization in Rural Bengaluru, RUAS - UAS JMC, Vol.13, Issue 01, pp. 1-10.
- Demonetisation Essay and Article – It's Impacts on the society, http://guidetoexam.com/demonetisation-essay-article/
- Demonetisation in Pakistan: Senate passes resolution to withdraw Rs 5000 note, Retrieved from http://indianexpress.com/article/world/demonetisation-in-pakistan-senate-passes-resolution-to-withdraw-rs-5000-note-4436576/
- Kasthuri, N. (2017). Impacts of Demonetisation on Indian Economy, Journal of Humanities and Social Science, pp. 29-30
- Kaul, M., & Mathur, P. (2017). Impact of digitalization on the Indian economy and requirement of financial literacy, Proceedings of International Conference on Recent Innovations in Engineering and Technology, Jaipur, India, 18th - 19th Feb'2017, pp. 100-104.
- Kiruthiga, V. & Magesh, R. (2016). Upshot of Demonetization in India, International Journal of Emerging Trends in Science and Technology, 3 (11), pp. 4788-4790.
- Kokila, V. & Ushadevi, R. (2017). The Impact of Demonetization on Retailing – An Analysis, International Journal of Commerce, Business and Management, Vol. 6, No.2, pp. 52-56.

- Krishnan, A. (2017), Demonetization Anniversary: Decoding the Effects of Indian Currency Notes Ban, Retrieved from https://economictimes.indiatimes.com/tdmc/your-money/demonetization-anniversary-decoding-the-effects-of-indian-currency-notes-ban/articleshow/61579118.cms
- Meher, B. (2017). Impact of Demonetization on NPA Position of Indian Banks, International Journal of Advance Scientific Research and Engineering Trends, 2 (1), pp. 1-7.
- Muthulakshmi, E. & Kalaimani, G. (2017). Impact of Demonetization on Indian Economy, Journal of Humanities and Social Science, pp.50-54.
- Muthulakshmi, E. (2017). Impacts of Demonetisation on Indian Economy- Issues & Challenges, Journal of Humanities and Social Science, pp.34-38.
- One year after demonetization – Has India eliminated 'black money'? , Retrieved from http://www.dw.com/en/one-year-after-demonetization-has-india-eliminated-black-money/a-41276486
- Preethi, S., & Sangeetha, V. (2017). Impact of Demonetization on Indian Economy, International Journal of Research in Economics and Social Sciences, Vol. 7 Issue 3, pp. 20~28.
- Sangeetha, S. (2017). Benefits of Demonetization: Rich and Poor, Journal of Humanities and Social Science, pp. 29-30.
- Santoshi, I. (2017). Constitutional validity of demonetization in India, International Journal of Law, Volume 3; Issue 1; Page No. 45-47.
- Sueniel (2017). Essay on Demonetisation in India – Notebandi Short Speech, Essay, Paragraph, Retrieved from https://teenatheart.com/short-speech-essay-paragraph-demonetization-article/
- Sunil (2017). Demonetization at glance in Indian scenario: A conceptual study, International Journal of Applied Research 2017, pp. 04-08.
- Tawade, P. (2017). Future and scope of cashless economy in India, IJARIIE, Vol-2 Issue-3, pp.177-181.
- The Indian Express, March 17, 2017, Anti-demonetisation experts like Amartya Sen stand exposed, says economist Jagdish Bhagwati, Retrieved from http://indianexpress.com/article/india/anti-demonetisation-experts-like-amartya-sen-stand-exposed-says-economist-jagdish-bhagwati-4573545/
- Veerakumar, K. (2017). A study on people impact on demonetization, International Journal of Interdisciplinary Research in Arts and Humanities, Volume 2, Issue 1, pp.9-11.
- Rao, G. (2000). Tax reform in India: achievements and challenges, Asia-Pacific Development Journal, Vol. 7, No. 2, pp. 59-73.
- Shah, S. & Joshi, N. (2017). Tax reform for developing viable and sustainable tax systems in India with special reference to GST, International Journal of Management, Volume 8, Issue 1, pp.119–126.
- Bernardi, L., & Fraschini, A. (2005). Tax system and tax reforms in India, Working paper no. 51, pp. 1-30.
- Rao, G. & Rao, R. (2006). Trends and Issues in Tax Policy and Reform in India, INDIA POLICY FORUM, pp. 55-100.

- Rupa, R. (2017). GST in India: An overview, International Education & Research Journal, 3 (2). pp.88-89.
- What is GST in India? Goods & Services Tax Law Explained (2018), Retrieved from https://cleartax.in/s/gst-law-goods-and-services-tax
- Goods and Service Tax (2017), Retrieved from https://en.wikipedia.org/wiki/Goods_and_Services_Tax_(India)
- https://www.gstindia.com/about/
- Chimoriya, B. (2018). Importance of Tax, Types and Objectives of Tax, Retrieved from https://www.wisenepali.com/2014/12/importance-of-tax-types-and-objectives.html
- https://www.bankbazaar.com/
- Vasal, V. (2017). How will GST impact the Indian economy, Retrieved from https://www.livemint.com/Politics/mNji15YJqkEF44MoNahNsL/How-will-GST-impact-the-Indian-economy.html
- Kashyap, K. (2017). The Four Benefits of the New Goods and Services Tax (GST) For Startups in India, https://www.forbes.com/sites/krnkashyap/2017/07/10/the-four-benefits-of-the-new-goods-and-services-tax-gst-for-startups-in-india/#553643531ef1
- https://qz.com/1245549/kalakriti-archives-rare-maps-reveal-how-indias-cartography-evolved-over-centuries/
- https://www.quora.com/Who-does-the-Goods-and-Services-Tax-GST-in-India-actually-favour
- https://cleartax.in/s/gst-analysis-and-opinions
- The Economic Times (Aug.11, 2017). How GST will impact a common man's budget, Retrieved from https://economictimes.indiatimes.com/news/economy/policy/how-gst-will-impact-a-common-mans-budget/articleshow/60011410.cms
- Kashyap, K. (2017). How Goods and Service Tax (GST) Impacts Five Key Sectors Of India's Economy, https://www.forbes.com/sites/krnkashyap/2017/07/20/how-goods-and-service-tax-gst-impacts-these-five-sectors-of-indias-economy/#66f0fdb6e83f
- http://www.obmworldwide.com/blog/advantages-and-disadvantages-of-vat/
- http://www.businessdictionary.com/definition/value-added-tax-VAT.html
- http://www.businessdictionary.com/definition/value-added-tax-VAT.html
- https://www.cakart.in/forum/answers/objectives-of-vat
- Value added tax (2018), Retrieved from https://en.wikipedia.org/wiki/Value-added_tax
- https://www.thebalance.com/value-added-tax-pros-and-cons-397673
- https://accountlearning.blogspot.com/2012/01/characteristics-of-value-added-tax-vat.html
- https://accountlearning.blogspot.com/2012/01/types-of-value-added-tax-vat.html
- https://accountlearning.blogspot.com/2012/01/principles-governing-value-added-tax.html

- Mulay, R. (2017). Taxation Objectives: Top 6 Objectives of Taxation, Retrieved from http://www.economicsdiscussion.net/government/taxation/taxation-objectives-top-6-objectives-of-taxation-discussed/17450
- Muley, R. (2017). Canons of Taxation: Meaning, Types and Characteristics, http://www.economicsdiscussion.net/government/taxation/canons-of-taxation-meaning-types-and-characteristics/17428
- Digital currency (2018). Retrieved from https://en.wikipedia.org/wiki/Digital_currency
- Cashless society (2018), Retrieved from https://en.wikipedia.org/wiki/Cashless_society
- What are the differences between regressive, proportional and progressive taxes? | Investopedia https://www.investopedia.com/ask/answers/042415/what-are-differences-between-regressive-proportional-and-progressive-taxes.asp#ixzz5CWk263MN
- http://www.economicsdiscussion.net/taxes/indirect-taxes/merits-and-demerits-of-indirect-taxes/12794
- Suman, S. (2017). Merits and Demerits of Direct Taxes, http://www.economicsdiscussion.net/taxes/direct-taxes/merits-and-demerits-of-direct-taxes/12798
- https://toughnickel.com/personal-finance/Advantages-and-Disadvantages-of-Direct-Taxes
- https://www.investopedia.com/terms/t/taxbase.asp#ixzz5CZG7c9Fh
- https://www.economicshelp.org/blog/2427/taxes/tax-tolerance/
- https://www.coursehero.com/file/p2ctf4q/Merits-of-Excise-Duty-or-Importance-of-Excise-Duty-1-Major-source-of-Government/
- https://www.deskera.in/gst-benefits-and-impact-on-indian-economy/
- Nihar, N. (2017). The Story from the Past: History of Goods and Service Tax, Retrieved from http://www.gstjockey.com/blog/the-story-from-the-past-history-of-goods-and-service-tax
- Thilagavathy, C. & Santhi, S. (2017). Impact and Importance of Cashless Transaction in India, Retrieved from https://zenodo.org/record/1001142#.WtHqkIhubIU
- https://www.quora.com/What-are-the-advantages-of-cashless-transaction
- Litvack, L.,& Vigne, S. (2017). Demonetisation in India and Emerging Challenges: A Report Delivered to the Department for the Economy, Northern Ireland and the Government of India by Queen's University Belfast and O.P. Jindal Global University. Belfast: Queen's University Belfast.
- Embracing the Digital Revolution Policies for Building the Digital Economy, February 2017, pp.1-33.
- Chaudhary, K., Singh, S., Subedi, N., Kaur, K., & Kour, M. (2017). Demonetization: Experiment Mean of Financial Inclusion, International Journal of Innovative Studies in Sociology and Humanities, Volume: 2, Issue: 2, pp.1-9.
- Sabnavis, M., Sawarkar, A., & Mishra, M. (2016). Economic consequences of demonetization of 500 and 1000 Rupee Notes, Economics: Policy View.

- Uke, L. (2017). Demonetization and its effects in India, SSRG International Journal of Economics and Management Studies, pp. 18-20.
- Katke, K., Kamat, A., &Kalal, M. (2017). Impact of Demonetization on Indian Automobile Industry: A Special Reference to Car Industry, International Journal of Scientific Engineering and Research, Volume 5 Issue 3, pp.71-74.
- Shah, A. (2017). Impact of Demonetization on Rural India, International Journal of Scientific and Research Publications, Volume 7, Issue 3, pp.220-223.
- Shirley, A. (2017), Impact of Demonetization in India, Special Issue Published in International Journal of Trend in Research and Development, National Conference on Impact of Indian 500 & 1000 Rupee Note Demonetisation (NCIRD-17), Organized by PG and Research Department of Commerce, Joseph Arts and Science College, Thirunavalur, Villupuram Dt, TamilNadu on 11th Feb 2017.www.ijtrd.com.
- Shendge, P., Shelar, B., and Kapase, S. (2017). Impact and Importance of Cashless Transaction in India, International Journal of Current Trends in Engineering & Research, Volume 3 Issue 4, pp.22-28.
- Beyes, P.& Bhattacharya, R. (2017). India's 2016 demonetisation drive: A case study on innovation in anti-corruption policies, government communications and political integrity, pp.2-6.
- Krishna, A. (2017). Demonetization in India: One More Rock in the River, p.154.
- Denis Abrazhevich." "Electronic Payment Systems: A User-Centered Perspective and Interaction Design", Proefschrift. -ISBN 90-386-1948-0NUR 788, 2004.
- Ailya Izhar, Aihab khan, Malik Sikandar Hayat Khiyal, 4Wajeeh Javed and Shiraz Baig , "Designing and implementation of Electronic Payment gateway for developing countries", journal of Theoretical and applied information technology, vol, 26 No. 230 April 2011.
- Yang Jing," "On-line Payment and Security of E-commerce". Proceedings of the 2009 International Symposium on Web Information Systems and Applications (WISA'09) Nanchang, P. R. China, May 22-24, 2009, pp. 046-050.
- Kaur, K.& Pathak, A. (2015). E-Payment System on E-Commerce in India, International Journal of Engineering Research and Applications, Vol. 5, Issue 2, (Part -1), pp.79-87.
- Sharif, M. (2016). Demonetization of Currency Notes: Significance and Challenges, International Journal of Innovative Research and Advanced Studies, Volume 3 Issue 12, pp. 60-63.
- Gaur, A.& Padiya, J. (2017). From Demonetisation to Digitization of Indian Economy: The Road Ahead, Proceedings of International Conference on Strategies in Volatile and Uncertain Environment for Emerging Markets July 14-15, 2017, pp. 598-605.
- Bansal, C. (2017). Impact of demonetization on Indian economy, International conference on innovative research in science, technology and management, 22-23 January 2017, p.128.
- Kaur, H., & Kaur, R. (2017). Impact of demonetization on FMCG sector, International Journal of Marketing & Financial Management, Volume 5, Issue 3, pp.27-32.

- E-commerce in India (2018), Retrieved from https://en.wikipedia.org/wiki/E-commerce_in_India
- Growth of E-Commerce in India (PDF Download Available). Available from: https://www.researchgate.net/publication/318280714_Growth_of_E-Commerce_in_India [accessed Apr 24 2018].
- E-commerce industry in India (2017), Retrieved from https://www.ibef.org/industry/ecommerce.aspx
- Russell, J. (2018), The future of e-commerce in India increasingly looks like an all-American affair, Retrieved from https://techcrunch.com/2018/04/23/the-future-of-e-commerce-in-india-increasingly-looks-like-an-all-american-affair/
- Dhananjay, B. & Chandra, S. (2015). The Electronic Banking Revolution in India, Journal of Internet Banking and Commerce, Retrieved http://www.icommercecentral.com/open-access/the-electronic-banking-revolution-in-india.php?aid=59261
- Gupta, S. (2018), Cyber-crime, Retrieved from https://www.myadvo.in/blog/cyber-crime-in-india/

Websites

- https://www.oberlo.com/ecommerce-wiki/ecommerce
- https://bizfluent.com/list-6023059-disadvantages-e-business.html
- https://medium.com/@briannawillsss/18-major-benefits-of-e-commerce-business-for-retailers-customers-in-2015-63c5fc87f679
- https://www.thebalancesmb.com/advantages-of-ecommerce-1141610
- https://cyberchimps.com/e-commerce-websites/
- https://en.wikipedia.org/wiki/Information_Technology_Act,_2000
- https://www.acorn.gov.au/learn-about-cybercrime
- https://www.ukessays.com/essays/information-technology/the-various-forms-of-e-banking-information-technology-essay.php
- https://www.cibc.com/en/student/student-life/benefits-of-online-banking.html
- http://www.indiacelebrating.com/essay/digital-india-essay/
- https://en.wikipedia.org/wiki/National_Automated_Clearing_House
- https://brainly.in/question/310745#readmore
- http://www.forbesindia.com/article/weschool/digital-revolution-in-the-indian-banking-sector/47811/1
- https://en.wikipedia.org/wiki/National_Payments_Corporation_of_India
- https://everythingfinanceblog.com/18570/top-5-benefits-core-banking-solutions-banks.html
- https://freebcomnotes.blogspot.com/2017/02/core-banking-introduction-meaning.html
- https://www.ukessays.com/essays/project-management/the-characteristics-of-internet-banking.php
- https://www.hdfcbank.com/personal/making-payments/fund-transfer/national-electronic-funds-transfer

- https://en.wikipedia.org/wiki/National_Financial_Switch
- https://en.wikipedia.org/wiki/Real-time_gross_settlement
- https://www.esds.co.in/blog/what-exactly-is-core-banking/#sthash.GvNNFSgS.dpbs

Index

M

N

O

P

R